Humane Leadership

For Beth & Mark,

thank you for

your friendship.

Humane Leadership

Tools to Engage, Empower, and Improve Performance

Stephen Bárczay Sloan

ISBN: 978-1-7348676-0-2
Printed in the United States of America

Humane Leadership Institute
humaneleadershipinstitute.org

Dedicated to the little girl
who changed everything

FSC
www.fsc.org
MIX
Paper from
responsible sources
FSC® C101537

Table of Contents

1

Hi.

In deciding to pick up this book, you accepted your role as a leader, to consider what "humane" might mean to you, to engage with your curiosity. Thank you.

In exchange for your curiosity, I offer a new relationship to your work, your team, your leadership, and maybe even to yourself.

Do you believe that our ways of leading ourselves and each other could be more fulfilling **and** more effective? I know we can do better.

In this book, I present a structured method for having performance improvement conversations that honor our shared values, humanity, and desire to produce excellent results. What I offer here, I learned the hard way.

Days in the Desert

Scottsdale, Arizona, the late 1990s.

I drive up between manicured lawns, palm trees and a backlit sign in front of a waterfall. The Phoenician resort looms like a stone temple at the foot of Camelback Mountain. I am here to attend an office supply industry conference billed as a "revolutionary step forward." The resort is certainly fancier than the midwestern airport hotels the office supply industry usually gathers in.

I walk through the gleaming lobby towards the opening party, greeting associates along the way. At that moment, I own three progressive companies in the industry and serve on the industry association board of directors. I am also chairman of the largest independent stationary business cooperative, formed to protect 1,000 family businesses from a Wall Street funded invasion by Office Depot, OfficeMax and Staples.

I've worked hard for twelve years to climb to these leadership positions. I am thirty-five years old, privileged, and gathering power rapidly in this odd corner of the world.

The poolside party on this balmy evening is like a dream. Energetic music thumps and the light of the pool dances across the assembled industry leaders chatting about golf and business. Young, fit women mingle with the middle aged men. The women chat warmly and smile as they pull tequila bottles from leather holsters slung low on their hips to pour into the men's upturned mouths.

Dazed, I order a beer and observe the spectacle.

The next morning, I sit in a strategy meeting of the cooperative's board before joining the hundreds of others to hear the keynote addresses. Loud music and flashing lights herald the entrance of file folder and paper clip titans as they stride on stage to congratulate themselves on their vision and endlessly skyrocketing sales charts.

The internet is revolutionizing how even copy paper and staplers are distributed, and young men shamelessly tout miraculous technologies that are destined to disrupt everything the older businessmen understand. "Of course, fine sir, with a not-so-modest investment, you can profit from the revolution yourself…."

Faces and logos flow across the stage while the graphs and egos all seem to bulge with boundless, manic success. The tempest in the office supplies teapot rages all day like an echo chamber of uncritical thinking, hubris and greed.

I listen with grave doubts because from my positions of leadership I understand that:

- Many challenges lurk beneath the glossy promise of new technologies.
- Most of the self-aggrandizing, flirtatious bonvivants are actually humble, married businesspeople.
- Many Cheshire cat executive smiles are masking manipulations and power grabs that will serve few and hurt many.
- A decade before, this very hotel was at the center of the savings and loan crisis, when it was seized by

> regulators and landed the builder in prison for fraud, racketeering, and conspiracy.

Here I am at the peak of my influence and success, after twelve years of grinding effort, attending a global forum of industry leaders with whom I share a lot of life focus but evidently little in terms of values, hosted at the scene of a huge white collar crime. I feel deeply disturbed.

That evening, as I drive out into the suburban desert, my thoughts spiral darkly downward. I am facing the intellectual and moral bankruptcy of everything I have worked so hard to achieve.

To break my silent spiraling, I turn on the car radio. My ears are filled with human voices rising and falling in a transcendent thirty-six part harmony, Ockeghem's *Deo Gratia.* The 500 year old beauty and order of that music reach deep inside me and uncover a long ignored spark.

My deepest values around truth and beauty are rekindled after being buried by years of hyper-focused striving.

From that moment, I've felt called to reweave my deepest values into my life and work.

Who am I to be leading this journey?

First, let's get real. I am a far from perfect leader.

I was a painfully introverted teen. In college, I forced myself to interact with others by becoming a realtor and making excruciating cold calls. The frameworks and tools in this book grew out of my experience of becoming a leader from an introverted, sensitive and highly distractible young man.

I became a fairly successful leader, but what's unique about my journey is that I paid close attention and took good notes on my experiments over the last thirty years.

To round out the picture, here's my leadership mea culpa:

- In my twenties I had 35 employees.
- While in the commercial office supply business, I got to speak with thousands of business owners, controllers, front-line leaders, and employees in a huge variety of industries.
- By my mid-thirties I had two businesses and a software startup. I worked hard, took big risks and sometimes couldn't take a paycheck myself.
- Along the way, I hired and fired a lot of people, including immediate family members.
- I was overly focused, short-tempered and on the verge of becoming completely cynical.
- I burned out.
- I sold what I could, closed up the rest, then I retreated to an island.
- I chopped wood, read, and held our babies by the woodstove for years.
- I look back on all the leadership actions I've taken and I feel something between ambivalence and disgust at my own shortsightedness and slow learning.

A few years after selling my own businesses, I was asked to consult for a successful entrepreneur facing a leadership crisis. Since that phone call, I have consulted for a wide variety of social and business entrepreneurs, led global and national sales and service teams, and helped global technology firms with strategic marketing, emerging technology strategy, and acquisitions.

In the process, I learned to feel and to think more deeply.

At one point on my journey, I found myself in a glass walled conference room just across the hall from the CEO and CFO's offices asking for $2 million more dollars for my business sales team.

I knew that underlying their obvious skepticism were the voices and values of their private equity bosses. How could I justify asking for that much money when the company was just emerging from bankruptcy?

The year before we'd sent two people to the hospital during our eight week "season" of 12 to 14 hours days, six days a week. I refused to accept that this was "just the way it is around here." I knew my team needed me to build a strong case and an even stronger action plan to both improve employee experience **and** deliver the results the board wanted.

To convince the executives and the board of my plan to stop treating our sales team as replaceable cogs in a machine, I knew I would need to draw on real data, solid models, and clear logic.

I started with a model tying employee experience to customer satisfaction and operating profits I'd found in the Harvard Business Review. To support the logic, I brought in the idea that managers should develop team members, not just drive them, based on real data and solid analytics from Google's Project Oxygen. Finally, I knew that I would need proof of bottom line results delivered by our sales team.

The CEO turned to me and said, "Show us what you've got." I presented models and frameworks as they sat back in their chairs, trying to hide their doubt behind blank expressions and folded arms. When I told them that the team had added $200,000 of sales above plan at no additional cost in the last 30 days using the sales approaches we'd created together, the arms unfolded and the questions started flowing.

Within a few days, the board approved the budget to rebuild the sales team and its workflow to dramatically improve both employee experience and sales results. Thus began my campaign to bring humane leadership to corporate America.

The Problems

As **leaders** we face a variety of challenges every day:

- The pressure to meet the organization's goals.
- The need to improve the performance of our all too human team.
- The moral ambiguities of power and our own integrity.

As **humans** we and our team members face a separate set of challenges:

- We earn our pay by working in often disempowering organizations.
- Our mental work disengages us from our bodies and deepest values.
- We feel the disappointment of our unmet need to work in a collaborative learning culture.

How can we create a culture of performance improvement and leadership that addresses all of the opportunities inherent in these problems?

Humane Leadership

Let's define terms:

Humane adj.

1. *Having or showing compassion or benevolence.*
2. *Branch of learning intended to have a civilizing or refining effect on people.*

Leadership n.

1. *The action of leading a group of people or an organization.*

Leading v.

1. *Cause (a person) to go with one by holding them by the hand or other method while moving forward.*
2. *Be a route or means of access to a particular place or in a particular direction.*
3. *Be in charge or command of.*
   a. *Organize or direct.*
   b. *Set a process in motion, start.*

"Be in charge" is the meaning of leadership that we habitually think of, but the first two meanings are also important. "Leading" in this book will be defined as the act of holding to move forward, organizing, directing, and setting in motion.

So "humane leadership" suggests that we hold responsibility for helping people and organizations better pursue shared goals while ensuring the journey consists of the compassionate refinement of talents, habits, character and skills.

How can we take on this responsibility without a shared set of values?

Humane Leadership Values

Humane leadership springs from three core values:

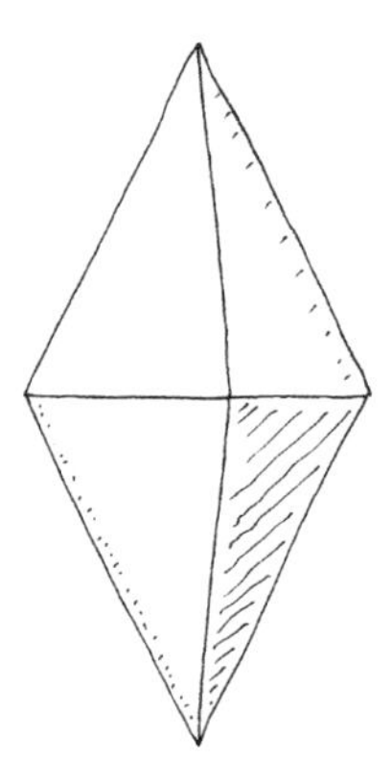

Fair Strength

Combining strength, clarity and beauty

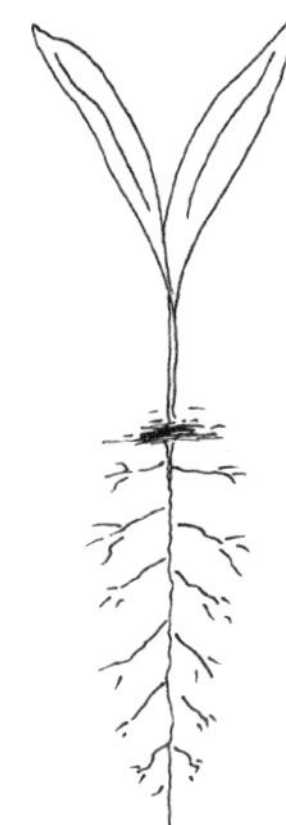

Generative Care

Offering nurturance to each person and moment

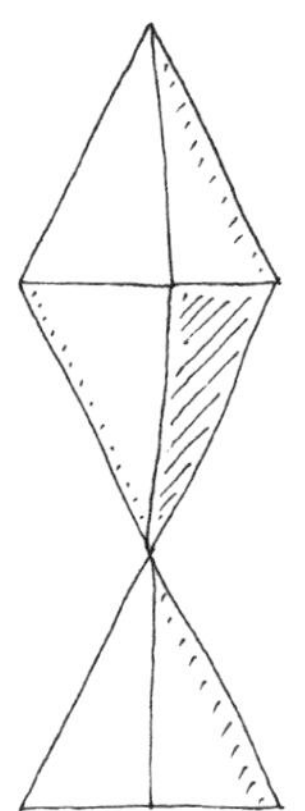

Wise Balance

Balancing strength and care

Fair strength. Leaders need to be strong, especially in the hardest moments. The leader is the one who, after group deliberation, steps forward and says, "Good thinking, let's go for option two. Come on, everybody, here we go!" That's our idea of a strong-in-a-crisis leader. That leader is like a diamond, beautifully strong, created under intense heat and pressure.

While decisive strength is important, it's not everything. A leader who is strong but unfair is ugly – more like a bully or a despot.

Humane leaders balance their strength with fairness. The word **fair** is interesting because it has at least a couple of meanings. One meaning is to be just, to do what's equitable for our community, our organization, and our earth.

But **fair** also means beautiful. Can we agree that strength can also be beautiful? There can be elegance in strength. It's not a bragging, self aggrandizing, immature strength, it's a certain confidence and savoir faire. Humane leaders have a beautiful strength that's subtle– it's only strong when it needs to be. It's measured, wise and serves as many as possible.

Generative care. Humane leaders practice generative care when they empower, edify and encourage. Humane leaders inspire care for each other and our highest values and aspirations. This generative care is the foundation of every thought and action they take. Without this care, we wouldn't be doing things for the right reasons. There needs to be an element of love for the work, for the people we're serving, for the people we're leading, and for our own hope and faith in humanity.

If we're not working from that place as a leader, we should ask ourselves if we should be leading at all.

Ideally, our organizations work within a culture of CARE which brings all the values and methods of humane leadership to life in service of employee experience, customer satisfaction, impact, and profitability. CARE is an acronym for:

- **Connect:** I feel connected at a human level, as a complex, sensitive, adaptive being.
- **Achieve:** I am experiencing the joy and rewards of accomplishment.
- **Respect:** I am respecting myself and others, as well as the materials, processes, and tools around me.
- **Emerge:** I am consciously choosing to develop my skills, attitudes and approaches through this work.

By using the tools and methods in this book, you can create a culture of CARE in your life, family and organization starting at the front line leader and team level. This will bring your employee experience, employment, investor, and market brands into alignment and integrity. Look on our website for a tool to support evaluating and refining your own culture in the CARE framework.

Wise balance. The diamond of our fair strength must rest upon balanced wisdom. Wisdom requires balancing:

- Our own needs and deeply held values.
- The competing needs of our team, our organization, and our shared social and natural ecosystems.

- Use of financial, natural, and time resources.
- The sharpness of our rationality and judgment with the care and nurturance of our shared humanity.

Every decision requires balancing competing values wisely. Every action reveals the relative wisdom and integrity of our lived values.

Leadership is not work for the faint of heart. This is work for people who care enough to make a difference and hold their own integrity at the same time. They are humane leaders – leaders who are humbled by their responsibility and dogged in their striving to live these values each day.

Redefining Work

Could the purpose of work extend beyond mere production of valuable goods and services in exchange for a paycheck?

In his book, *Small is Beautiful*, E.F. Schumacher, a British economist who studied Gandhi's thinking, proposed that work has three purposes:

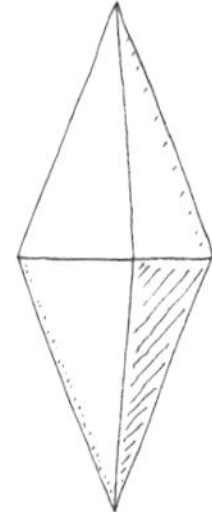

Develop our capabilities so we can perform better and contribute more.

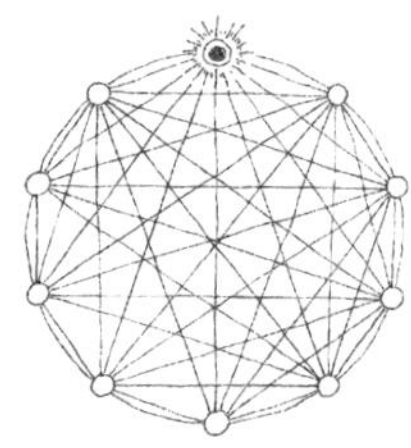

Transcend ourselves through collaboration with others.

Create goods and services relevant to our mission or plan.

This is not some esoteric idea. Peter Drucker, one of the great management thinkers of the 20th century wrote that leadership is less "magnetic personality" and more about "lifting a person's vision to higher sights, the raising of a person's performance to a higher standard, the building of a personality beyond its normal limitations."

Following Drucker's model we can learn to better engage, empower and improve the performance of all our team members. This model also allows us to see when we can create an opening for someone to build their own leadership skills. This is the heart of success and satisfaction as a leader, seeing every moment as a chance to edify someone you care about.

How to Benefit From This Book

This is a practical, comprehensive guide to performance improvement that provides tools for human development at work, in community and in families.

The approach is simple:

- Collaboratively review performance.
- Identify opportunities for improvement.
- Design experiments to make improvements.
- Evaluate progress and refine experiments.

Of course, the book offers much more than just a simple approach. We introduce a framework in chapter two so anyone can quickly evaluate performance issues and opportunities for improvement. In chapter three we explain how to effectively host a performance review meeting and in chapter four, we explain some of the concepts underlying these methods.

The balance of the book is a primer and reference for the many challenges and opportunities you will discover in working with the humane performance improvement practices you've learned. Chapters five and six examine the wide variety of challenges that we may bring to the performance improvement discussion. Chapters seven through eleven offer deeper understandings and tools to empower improvements in motivation, time and authority, clarity of expectations, and development of capabilities. Chapter twelve looks at the implications of the humane leadership approach for our lives and organizations.

These practical approaches will add power and nuance to whatever performance evaluation processes your organization already uses. The Performance Wisdom Jig in the next chapter helps leaders dig more deeply into situations your existing process uncovers and helps them co-create experiments to improve results. Of course, our approach can stand alone if your existing frameworks need an upgrade.

A new framework is the easy part, how can we create real, lasting change in performance levels?

How Change Happens

A theory of change is a set of assumptions about how change happens in our organizations, ourselves, or the larger society. Years working with teams has refined our theory of change to make it both practical and personal.

Our theory of change is **practical** because it focuses leaders on helping individuals experiment to create measurable performance improvements. Our theory of changes is based on the ideas of:

- **Service profit chain**– Developed at Harvard Business School, this framework links employee experience to retention, customer satisfaction, net profits, enterprise value, and real community impacts.
- **Earned influence**– Leaders must earn the right to lead their teams. We developed a model to support leaders in earning influence by being relevant, unique and visible, based loosely on philosopher Bertrand Russel's thoughts on power.
- **Conscious creativity**– Humane performance improvement assumes that we can choose our thoughts and actions based on free will and wisdom.
- **Thought and action**– We believe that changes of thought naturally lead to changes of behavior. Improved performance will create a positive feedback loop that makes the improved behavior habitual. This is based in first principles of cognitive behavioral therapies in psychology.

Our theory of change is **personal** because we believe that change happens one individual human being at a time, rather than to abstracted groupings of humans we call teams or organizations.

- **Each human is a leader,** if only of themselves. Each one of us possesses our own self-leadership laboratory. How humane and effective are you in your self leadership? Can you learn to better coordinate the light and dark forces of your own human nature? Hat tip to Plato and Socrates.

- **Values power change.** Our lives are created out of our values (fairness, strength, caring, wisdom, avoiding conflict, pursuing fame and fortune, maintaining safety, etc.). Our values are based on our sense of hope and faith in our own identity and potential. Acting in alignment with our values can be the source of our empowerment. Shift this relationship, shift your results.

- **Mindful attention leads to edification.** As we seek to see the reality of the people and the world around us in each moment, we become aware of our opportunities to edify ourselves and our team members.

More than being justified by some great end result, this theory of change allows us to hold our integrity as human beings who value reason, self-determination, moral virtue and human rights.

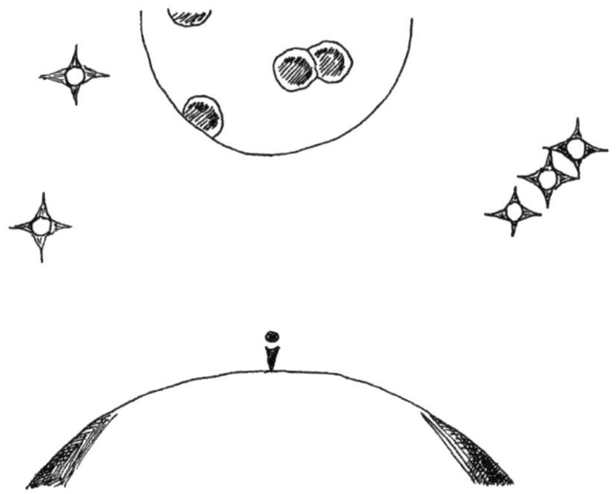

Be humble for you are made of earth,
Be noble for you are made of stars

— Serbian Proverb

But how do we make this change happen?

To internalize and make use of wisdom, we need to practice shaping our own thoughts and actions.

Wisdom Jigs: Tools to Improve Thinking

Buckminster Fuller wrote that the best way to teach a person a new mindset was to "...give them a tool, the use of which will lead to new ways of thinking."

We created wisdom jigs to help you and your team improve your thinking, transform your performance, and create winning new habits.

jig n. *A device that holds a piece of work and guides the tools operating on it.*

A jig is a tool to help you produce an intended result, to eliminate variables of position, angle, etc. The handheld pencil sharpener may be one of the simplest jigs you've used. The sharpener holds a blade at a precise angle and depth relative to the pencil lead and casing. Simply twist and you get a sharp pencil consistently.

Using wisdom jigs can give us a variety of related benefits:

Wisdom

- **Proven** thinking that's been tested over many years across a diverse set of people, cultures and eras.
- **Knowledge** that reveals the world as experts see it.

Jigs

- **Help** us make better decisions and gain valuable experience more quickly and with less risk.
- **Create** lasting change by upgrading our mental models and habits of thought and action.
- **Offer** an experience of rational thought and conscious development of our own hypotheses and thinking to motivate further learning.
- **Build** confidence in our own thinking and creativity based on the insights and actions we generate.

The best thinkers of our species have left signs and diagrams, manifestos and exhortations. Wisdom jigs help us internalize some of their learnings. So, may our patterns of thought be a conscious choice, not an unconscious habit.

We can choose our thought patterns out of fear, forget to choose at all, or we can begin to experiment with leading ourselves and each other more wisely and humanely.

> Life is a sum of all your choices.
>
> — Camus

As leaders, we can offer people the experience of choosing their own mental models, habits and experiments to optimize their results. This process lets us each become part of a self-teaching organism– a self-generated, self-refining intelligence.

Now, that is humane leadership.

We will support your humane leadership journey by offering all the wisdom jigs mentioned in this book as free PDF templates on our website. These mental models have been gifts to us and our clients so we are happy to make them gifts to you and your associates.

Notes on Quotes and Sources

As you travel with me through this book, you will notice that the quotes and citations are mostly from the work of dead white males.

I confess that I am a cisgender male of European decent, born at the tail end of the baby boom, who was raised in some privilege during times of relative peace and plenty. I also admit to a philosophical, analytical and historical approach to life.

I am aware of and humbled by the many challenges people face every day with diversity, equity and inclusion. I am aware of the many good people and efforts working to rectify, to the extent possible, the structural challenges in our society.

In building this book, I carefully considered including a more diverse set of quotes and references. In the end, reaching into what was, for me, unfamiliar territory felt more like appropriation and inclusion-washing than an authentic expression of my own experiences. So, I included the mostly dead white men that I have naturally gravitated towards in my very partial self education. I am happy that our children will be more diversely educated than I am. I consider that progress.

And yet, I believe the wisdom available in these pages can still empower emerging leaders no matter their circumstances. Humanity is us, all of us, and therefore humane leadership includes anyone and everyone who's prepared to lead themselves and others. Leadership includes every starting point and every next step. This includes you, if you would like to be included. It's my hope that by deconstructing my own experience of how power is created and used that I can make power more accessible to you and anyone else committed to using it for good.

Wisdom transcends our differences. May you find some reflected rays of light here.

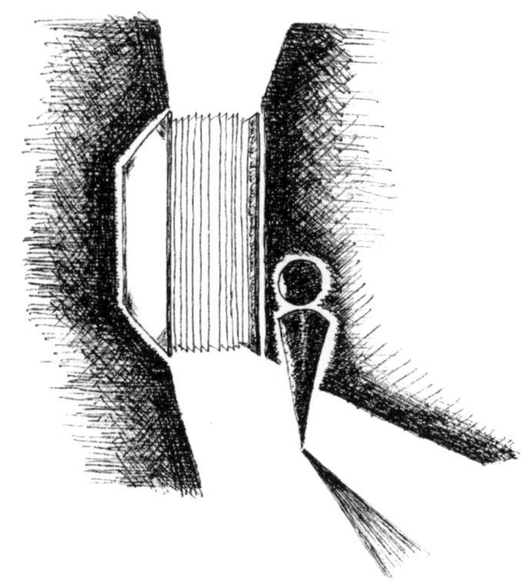

I hope you will accept this gift in the spirit in which I created and now offer it. Take what empowers you and please, leave the rest.

The Illustrations

OK, so what's the story with these simple drawings?

I hope the illustrations I drew make the book more relatable– they come unfiltered from my imagination into your experience. May they invite you into moments of clarity.

I also hope that the words and images here create an opening for you to bring more of your inner, protected self, more of your creativity, and more of your desire to express what's true for you into your working life.

Creating this book has been a wonderfully empowering, expressive and healing process for me. I hope it serves something wonderful in you.

Further Reading

At the end of each chapter, I list works that influenced my thinking or were mentioned. A few are business books, but most are books from the humanities– literature, history and philosophy. While it may seem inefficient, being tumbled in the kaleidoscope of the humanities helps us become more curious, compassionate, humble, and wise humans and leaders.

- Drucker, *Management: Tasks, Responsibilities, Practices,* 1973
- Fuller, see *Operating Manual for Spaceship Earth,* 1969 or *Critical Path,* 1981
- Plato, Allegory of the Charioteer, *Phaedrus Dialogue*
- Russell, Power: *A New Social Analysis,* 1938
- Sasser, et al, "Putting the Service Profit Chain to Work," Harvard Business Review, 1994
- Schumacher, *Small is Beautiful,* 1973

2

The single most valuable idea I learned in business school is P(MOCA), a model of the essential elements of performance. The model is an extension of the famous AMO model focused on **Ability, Motivation** and **Opportunity**. I added the leader's greatest lever, **Clarity** of expectations. The MOCA model has made my life, my work, and my leadership more fruitful and satisfying almost every day since I learned it.

This tool can help you overcome your own and others' shortcomings, confusion, and disengagement in a repeatable, collaborative, connective process. In our model, performance is a function of four variables:

- **M**otivation
- **O**pportunity
- **C**larity of Expectations
- **A**bility

I use the mnemonic P(MOCA), pronounced, "p-MO-ka," to remember the variables. We've reversed the order of the letters in the illustrations for reasons that will become clear in just a bit.

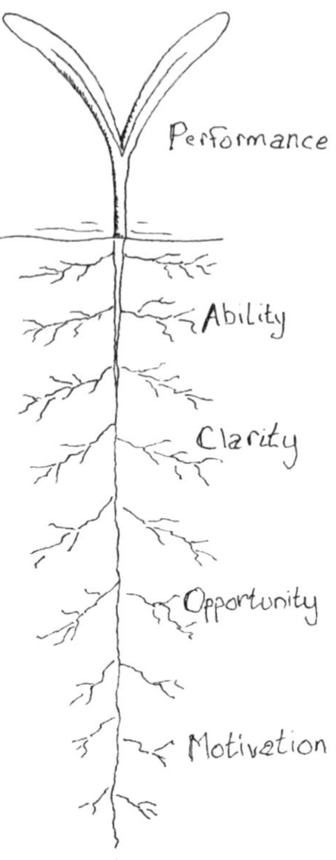

I'll explain the model with a track and field event, the high jump. In the high jump, the performance goal is to leap over a bar set as high as possible without knocking it down.

Motivation is required to run and jump over that bar. You may want to beat your personal record or qualify for a meet. You may have a drill sergeant coach or a tiger parent spurring you on.

Opportunity is the permission, authority, time, energy, and consciousness required to perform. In the high jump, when it's your turn, you have permission to try to jump over the bar. In a business setting, you may have the time to complete the work and the authority to take the actions, use the resources, and make the decisions required. However, you may lack the energy or focus to perform excellently on any particular day.

Clarity of expectations in the high jump is easy. You start here, you run, and you launch your body over the bar. The bar makes it perfectly clear how high you should try to jump.

If you knock the bar down three times in a row, you're out of the competition. Those are the rules. In business, the goals, methods, and rules are less clear and the search for meaningful measures of success can occupy a lot of time and attention.

Ability is a combination of talent, training and tools. You may be physically ideal for high jumping, you may practice the best techniques with a great coach, you may have excellent shoes. In business, the abilities, training, and tools you need are more complex, including analytical and emotional intelligence, technical training and sophisticated software or manufacturing equipment.

OK, we have a clear model for performance, but how do we put it to use?

The Performance (MOCA) Jig

Use this wisdom jig anytime you want to assess your own or someone else's performance at work or in your personal life.

In my experience, P(MOCA) is almost alchemical in its ability to transform the emotional energy of frustration around subpar performance into shared clarity, learning, alignment, and positive action.

Here is a sample completed first section of the jig to give you an idea of how this might work. Bulleted short sentences describing your findings are sufficient as long as they clearly capture the essence of what you think.

Performer: *Devon Webb* Role: *Web Dev*

Analysis by: *Leigh Dehr* Date: *dd / mm / yy*

Current, As-is Performance Analysis

Performance

- Not great. Seems to be maximizing client value and unstructured time at the expense of firm profits

Motivation Sources

- Low, seems to be focused on minimizing effort while maximizing praise from clients
- No worries about external accountability from the boss

Opportunity

- Yes, could be used more effectively

Clarity of Expectations

- Yes via retainer hour budgeted and client project statements of work
- Unclear measures of firm profit contribution expectations and actuals
- Unclear priorities for time outside of client retainer hours

Ability

- Labor intensive time tracking process and systems
- Loose to no time planning process

Before you begin working with this wisdom jig with a teammate or on yourself, I suggest you set the stage for collaboration. Ensure that your work/setting is:

- **Safe and non-judgmental**– we are seeking opportunities for improvement, not finding fault.
- **Collaborative**– working together to find insight and opportunity will lead everyone higher, faster. Call out the possibility that this could be seen as a confrontation or an opportunity to demean, demand, or even save. Discuss what agreements you can make to notice and avoid those patterns if they begin to emerge.
- **Experimental**– we are looking to discover how we might adjust the levels of the MOCA variables to give us measurably better performance.
- **Learning-focused**– our goal is to use this analysis and design process to learn as much as possible from the performance improvement experiments we've designed together.

People want to be held accountable. The key to doing this with some psychological safety is to take it out of blame and nit picking. If possible, sit at a round table, side by side, and look at the tool together. Ask, "Okay, what happened?"

Chapter three is all about how to set the stage and use the wisdom jig in a meeting. Now let's look at the jig itself.

Performer: Role:

Analysis by: Date:

Current, As-is Performance Analysis

Performance

Describe the performance you have witnessed. What worked and what didn't?

Motivation Sources

Internal and external motivators and how consistent they are at inspiring desired actions

Opportunity

Time and authority to actually do the work in the optimal way

Clarity of Expectations

Knowing the exact desired outcome and everything required to create it

Ability

Talent, skills, training and tools required by the job

Design the To-be State

Adjustments and experiments planned to improve future performance

Future Performance Vision

Motivation Sources

Opportunity

Clarity of Expectations

Ability

Download a PDF version of the Performance Wisdom Jig from the Humane Leadership website wisdom jigs page.

How to Use This Performance Wisdom Jig

You might consider trying the jig out on your own performance as a leader to gain familiarity, confidence and humility before trying it on others.

Assess Current Performance

Starting at the top of the page, describe the **performance** you have witnessed. Be observant and objective like a scientist. Try to get into the details about what worked and what did not. Be specific and concise. For colleagues, more detail is probably better. Of course, be sensitive to how what you write might land with the person; be clear and constructive while maintaining integrity and depth of observation. This should be descriptive, not judgmental writing.

In the **Motivation** section, make notes of what you have noticed about the person's motivation.

- Is it high or low?
- Does it seem to be internal or externally driven? Is it more fear-based or hope-based?
- Does it seem aligned with the values of your organization and the goals of the project?
- Is there inconsistency between stated motivations and motivations in practice?
- What specific behaviors lead you to these impressions?

In the **Opportunity** section, make notes of what you notice about opportunities to improve time management and self-empowerment in pursuit of strong performance.

- Did the person allow themselves enough time and use it wisely?
- Was their time their own to schedule or was it controlled by others?
- Did they have and use the authority to make the decisions and take the actions required to perform well?
- Did the person have the creative opportunity to contribute to the what, how, when, and where of their work?

In the **Clarity of Expectations** section, make notes about the person's clarity (or lack thereof) about the expected performance.

- Were there clearly defined deliverables, expected activities, behaviors, outcomes and due dates?
- Were there details missing that they could have clarified on their own?
- Where did the lack of clarity come from?
- Did the lack of clarity start at the outset or creep in along the way?

In the **Ability** section, note anything about the person's ability to perform well.

- Did they have the talent, tools, and training required to perform well?
- What was missing?
- Did they try to make do rather than request the tools and training they needed?

- What could they have requested from others to support their own success?

Envision Better Performance

On the next page, think about which variables you might experiment with to perform better next time.

Start at the top of the To-be State page and describe the improved performance you desire. Be as specific as possible and make the improvements measurable and time-bound in your description. If you're doing this with another person, allow for discussion of and alignment on this new vision.

Each of the four variables now become levers that the subject gets to experiment with.

In the second section, note any ideas about the motivations that would inspire improved performance and how the person might get greater creative ownership of their own motivation.

In the third section, note ideas for improving time use and assuming and delegating authority.

Next, clarify expectations about the desired outcomes and ideas for keeping those desired outcomes in mind in the process of doing the work.

Finally, note any improvements to abilities that would make a difference.

- How could the team member extend their own capabilities by gathering better tools and training?

- Is it possible that the person simply does not have the innate talents required to perform well? How can you design an experiment to know for sure?
- If they don't have the native ability required, can you design a bridge to a role that's a better fit for this person? Completing this wisdom jig in collaboration with an employee can clearly and naturally open that often challenging conversation. More on that in the next chapter.

Design Experiments to Improve Performance

Look across all the bullet points you have written and circle those with the highest potential for improving performance.

How might you experiment with two or three of those?

Which experiment might drive the biggest impacts most quickly?

Evaluate the benefit to effort ratio of each potential experiment. How can you mix a few quick wins with progress towards bigger challenges?

Look at what can be started now to create the most impactful, long-term improvements.

Agree on and design your experiments. Much more on this in the coming chapters.

Applications and Implications

This Performance Wisdom Jig is a deceptively simple yet powerful structure for one-on-one meetings with team members.

It is also very useful for our own self leadership performance development work.

Self leadership is critical to developing our humane leadership of others. If we don't look carefully at ourselves, we may be tempted to become cynical and critical of those around us.

Having a standardized, shared conceptual framework for assessing performance allows us to focus on the drivers of improvement across time rather than looking for excuses, blame, or making each other feel better. Having examined our own performance challenges prepares us to collaborate with others on theirs.

The very structure of the Performance Wisdom Jig transforms conflict into creative collaboration.

Using a wisdom jig to empower a person to think clearly about what is and what isn't working, and then to devise their own experiments to improve their performance can be a revolutionary act that benefits the worker, the leader, the organization, and its stakeholders. The rest of the book focuses on how to realize these benefits for yourself and your team.

3

Holding Form in Performance Improvement Meetings

Humane leaders ensure productive, invigorating meetings by holding form. They host a creative, deliberative conversation rather than trying to dominate or drive the group. Meetings without form are usually a mess and whoever brings the necessary purpose, focus and structure to the conversation is the de facto leader. Many of us need to step into this role more often and more expertly. Holding form goes far beyond agenda setting.

The dynamics of an interaction are often shaped by physical and social forms. Are we going into the interaction thinking that it is a confrontation, a mea culpa, or a time to humor the big boss with a fragile ego and a loose grip on reality? Is one person speaking from behind a podium, invisibly from a loudspeaker, whispering in your ear, or raging from behind a big desk? Each of these forms will shape your experience.

As humane leaders, we want to create a form that holds safe human connection along with focused, balanced and purposeful collaboration.

A performance improvement meeting will be a dialogue between two humans seeking to identify the tensions between what is true now and what's ideally next, and then designing how to step toward opportunities for improvement. This potentially stressful dialogue will be easier and more effective if we are aware of its social, physical, emotional and mental elements.

Social Form

Any conversation around performance will have some social hierarchy underpinning it. Even among social peers, there will be a hierarchy unconsciously established based on perceived level of accomplishment, or what Ray Dalio calls a person's "believability."

To effectively, authentically collaborate, we must find a way to level the playing field for a few moments. One way to do this is to focus on a shared search for truth, using clear experiments to test hypotheses.

We can begin this process by reviewing the goals for the meeting and how the Performance Wisdom Jig can support them:

- Discover what's true about current performance or As-Is state.

- Collaborate to design an improved To-Be state.
- Agree on how we might run experiments to test our performance improvement hypotheses.

To break down inherited social structures will take great clarity and care. Some people may bring their own legacy of hierarchical, possibly abusive, forms of leadership, authority, and performance evaluation. "You can do better than that! Try again! Now!"

Others may bring a warm, soft, but never demanding experience of performance leadership. "Everyone gets a trophy!" The world of work calls us to clearer, cleaner, more compelling relationships with expectations and accountability.

To start, ask the team member to complete the Performance Wisdom Jig on their own performance before the meeting. This thoughtful self evaluation will give the person time to orient to the goal, the model and the process. It will allow them to choose how honest and creative they want to be with themselves and with you. Be sure they have at least 20 uninterrupted minutes to focus on their self evaluation.

Of course, you will also take time to give the person and their performance your attention by making notes on their performance and the variables that went into creating it. Also, work on your own ideas for potential experiments.

First, consider the quality of the team member's current performance, making bullets in the top section. Ideally, you will have some thoughts on:

- What measures have been met, which have not?

- What is the quality of their work product and of their collaboration with the team and clients?
- How motivation, opportunity, clarity of expectations, and ability contributed to their current performance.

Continue on to the next page to think about the improved performance you would like to see from them. Finally, think about experiments you think might help them improve. Now, you are prepared to collaborate.

This prep work will allow each of you to come to the meeting prepared to collaborate on an even playing field. But, to really create a collaborative situation will require more form setting.

Physical Form

Considering physical form is quite practical and humane because it affects all parts of our humanity. For me, this starts with my physical size. I am a huge man, 6′6″ tall and, well, not slender. To host a conversation, I choose to sit and give my collaborators space so they can feel safe with me. The goal is to create a circle of intimacy, safety, honesty, and creativity with the other person.

To start, get out from behind your desk. I choose a round conference table if possible, somewhere quiet and private, in a peaceful space in which intimacy can grow. If only angular tables are available, sit on either side of a corner so that you can be as close to shoulder to shoulder as possible while not actually sitting side by side. This makes it easy to share papers and to look each other in the eye when that's called for.

Chairs should be solid, similar or the same (no hierarchy of throne, please) and comfortable, but not cushy or reclining. The chairs should facilitate shared work at the table so they should ideally be narrow and without arms so that you can lean in to work together.

Another important aspect of physical form is the presence or absence of computers. Because this conversation is about and between humans, I avoid having a computer at the table if at all possible. Even phones should be silenced and put out of sight.

Reference materials and thinking tools, including a blank copy of the Performance Wisdom Jig for note taking, are ideally printed on paper. Yes, paper has costs, but the quality of this conversation determines the trajectory of your team member's career, your quality as a leader, and the success of your organization. Let's focus on direct human collaboration and forget the distractions of the digital world for a few moments.

The quality and substance of your conversation are what matter here, not the data; so don't do data entry when you are collaborating. Take a photo of your handwritten notes later if you need a digital record of your work.

Now that the physical stage is comfortable, focused and collaborative, it's time to turn our attention to creating a safe emotional space.

Emotional Form

The emotional form you set as leader is even more important than the physical, though they are intertwined. The emotional form setting starts well before you send the invitation. Be aware of what your recent (or even long passed) interactions might bring into the room as you seek to collaborate. How can you clear the emotional space to allow trust into the present conversation if you have had challenging interactions in the past?

We must begin by addressing any lack of trust. Patrick Lencioni, in *The Five Dysfunctions of a Team*, cites trust as the foundation for functional teamwork.

Trust is built slowly and destroyed quickly, so if there are trust issues in your relationship, it is probably best to:

- Acknowledge the past.
- Open space for the person to express any concerns or agenda items they have on their mind.
- Set an intention that this conversation begins to rebuild trust in your relationship.

Fear of conflict is the second dysfunction Lencioni identifies and is very important to address.

Check in with your emotions around your relationship with the person. Are you frustrated, disappointed or downright angry with them? Do your best to return to the present by writing, meditating, walking or whatever works for you. Then, start your meeting with the person by:

- Acknowledging that you had feelings that the person may have sensed in the past.

- Acknowledging that those feelings may have come across inappropriately.
- Stating your intention that, today, you are setting aside those feelings so you can work together with fairness and clarity to create something better.

A final note on the emotional setting; add warm water.

Holding a cup of warm liquid can open a person's heart and mind. Check out the research from the National Institutes of Health by searching, "Experiencing Physical Warmth Promotes Interpersonal Warmth."

Offering someone tea or coffee is a non-threatening way to invite them into a comfortable conversation. Offering a warm beverage also engages the norm of reciprocity, which inspires us naturally to respond generously when a gift is given. The norm of reciprocity states that if we are welcoming, forthcoming and vulnerable, the person we're with is more likely to reciprocate by being open as well.

Mental Form: Intention

Now, it's time to set the actors in motion on the stage we've set, but we must create the mental form to ensure that the collaboration yields the excellent performance and bottom-line results we desire.

First, clearly state the intention of the conversation. For instance, "Today, we'll work together to understand your performance, find what's working, and design an experiment that might make things even better."

It is important to create a time frame as well. You might say, "We have an hour, which I would like to break into three 20-minute blocks, matching the sections of the jig. We'll assess current state, envision next level, and design experiments."

As you engage with the mental form, return briefly to the emotional form by genuinely revealing your own humanity. Humane leaders can share without diminishing their authority simply by acknowledging the challenges of the moment: "I must admit, it feels a bit artificial to be sitting here talking about performance with you. It's not like any of us are perfect. We all have disconnects between our intentions and our actions. This challenge is as old as humanity. But, let's see what we can figure out together."

Acknowledging our shared challenges allows us to hold compassion with this person and still bring our full analytical capacity to disconnects between intention, action and results.

Then we step into collaboration by asking if they have any questions or items they would like to add to the agenda. Handle those first if they are of manageable size. If the items they mention open huge issues or seem like digressions, set another time to handle those topics right then and there. "Let's talk about those at 3pm on Thursday. I will send you an invitation." Make yourself a note to set the meeting right then. This will take just a moment, but will clear the balance of your time together of any mental or emotional obstacles.

Intentional Attention

As the conversation begins, relax and move your attention off of yourself and onto your team member. Keep it there; really allow yourself to see and hear them without your usual filters and assumptions in the way. Your mindfulness practice may be of great benefit here.

Heidi Gehman, a theology professor, explained intentional attention to me this way:

> Iris Murdoch said the primary moral work for human beings is to try to see the world outside of that egoistic perspective, and that required what she called "attention."
>
> Her idea of attention being that we have to actually **try** to see the world. It doesn't naturally come to us because again we have these filters on. She felt that if we can attend to individual realities outside of ourselves and really see them as valuable in and of themselves, that is the true way to see them distinctively.
>
> So, she said, we have to focus on individual human beings, because each individual human being is a unique creature. We can't just go around looking at everybody saying, "I know who these people are, they're driven by their own motives and I'm going to treat them as competition."

> You have to notice individual human beings in their own right and value in order to be able to treat them morally correctly– in order to be able to really respond to them as a human being. It's a claim that vision or attention is the primary moral act.

The quality of your calm, intentional attention is the greatest gift you can develop and give because:

> One of the deepest longings of the human soul is to be seen.
>
> — John O'Donohue

To offer your intentional attention, listen carefully to what your teammate is saying and ask questions about:

- Words that they use that you may not understand.
- Their own, deeper definitions of loaded words like: work, success, happiness and love.
- Assumptions that they have made about how things are connected or how things work.
- Logical next steps, extensions, or edge cases to what they are talking about.
- Their experiences and learnings from what they share.

By practicing intentional attention, the quality of your conversations will improve dramatically and so will your team member's sense of engagement.

For more on the powerful gift of intentional attention, search on "intentional attention interview with Heidi Gehman" and watch Krista Tippet's interview with David Whyte on "The Conversational Nature of Reality" in which they discuss the power of beautiful questions.

Collaborative Analysis of the As-Is State

Once you've carefully met the person and set your intentions for the meeting, start discussing their self evaluation of the status quo on their Performance Wisdom Jig. I recommend having a fresh copy of the Wisdom Jig available to capture notes from your discussion.

Ask your collaborator to read the notes they made on their own performance and the elements that created it. As you listen, look for overlap in what you both identified as the important facts of their performance. Note any differences in your analyses to be sure they are addressed in the flow of conversation. Be curious to see how the team member addresses or avoids what, to you, seem like the critical drivers of their performance. Appreciate all the positives you can, but do not shy away from addressing pain points, working from your fairest strength, your most generative care, and your most balanced wisdom.

Collaboration Basics

The key to collaboration here is to ask them for their thoughts first. This is surprisingly hard for many caring, action-oriented leaders who want to jump in and offer expert clarity and advice. Ideally, the person will unfold a clear, complete, self-generated analysis of their own performance.

Not everyone will. To those who need some help, offer support by asking questions– don't rescue them or do the analysis for them. This is an opportunity for you to help them deepen their thinking skills as well as gain courage in looking clearly at themselves and their work.

Don't feel compelled to affirm or correct every little part of the person's analysis. That can start to feel patronizing or mechanical. Maybe nod, say, "Hmm," and keep moving. Collaboration doesn't mean repetition and affirmation. It means meaningful dialogue in search of the truth, so only add what is missing, e.g. "I agree that your motivation seemed a bit low, but I wonder about its source as well. What do you find motivating?"

You will also be learning a lot about the person's ability, character, and sense of safety with you by seeing how clear, honest, and courageous they are when left to their own devices. This will be revealing of their level of engagement with their job as well as their willingness and ability to discuss challenging topics. You cannot accept avoidance or lazy analysis. You must pursue the truth about a teammate's performance gently, but inexorably; that is your job.

When you have people who avoid, try to distract, are extra agreeable and full of mea culpas and promises, see chapters five and six on challenging situations. For now, we will stay on the happy path of the engaged team member who wants to creatively collaborate.

Once the team member has offered all of their own thoughts, you can deepen their analysis based on your notes and any new questions that arose. Acknowledge the quality and depth of their self analysis. Then, respond by adding or extending where your analysis differs from theirs.

Do not simply read all of your notes on their performance as that fails to incorporate and reinforce what you just learned from them. This respects the work they have done and the risk they have taken in sharing their self analysis with you.

Hold focus carefully until the analysis is complete. Agree on the definitions of the words used, the measures cited, the key drivers of the performance, as well as both contributors and detractors from great work.

After about 20 minutes of exploring current performance, ask, "Do you feel like we have a clear understanding of the current situation?" Once you both feel clear and complete, move on to creating a vision of the To-Be state.

Designing the To-Be State

In this next portion of the meeting we co-design a humane and higher performance To-Be state.

Start in the top section and ask the team member to describe what they had listed as To-Be performance on their self-evaluation. Notice how thoughtful, rigorous and clear their ideas are. Discuss how your envisioned To-Be performance differs from what they wrote. Co-design the To-Be state to be as clear and measurable as possible, while considering the needs of the person and the team.

By focusing on needs, the employee can bring more of themselves into the conversation. We are not just working brains–we have bodies, emotions and values too. This brings the core idea of human-centered design into your creation of what's next.

For instance, as I write this I become aware of my very real needs for an ergonomically suitable writing desk and chair, I feel the pull of my child in the other room, my body's need for movement and exercise (I've been writing for almost 3 hours now), my emotional need to feel like I have had a productive day, etc. As a humane leader, you offer your team member permission to bring in more (if not all) of their needs to the conversation. Of course, some people's needs can overwhelm the need to get work done. We will address this and other challenges in chapter six.

You and your organization have needs as well. Usefully, you can add energy to the team member's clear analysis of their own needs by asserting the needs of the team. When you say, "We need x done by tomorrow," the person will naturally push back with, "Well, maybe, but I need a, b and c in order to do that!"

The information in this push back is gold for you as a leader. You were just given a clear statement of things to consider adding to your list of improvement projects. Every need and excuse from a team member can be converted by you into improved team performance.

On challenging days in leadership, I think of performance improvement as an exercise in excuse elimination. You tell me why you cannot do what needs to be done and I will remove those obstacles from your path **and** from your list of excuses.

Over time, most if not all excuses are eliminated and performance and quality of the team improves. This is a form of rigorous servant leadership. Those who are more committed to their excuses than performing well will find their own way out the door.

Work through the variables in the remaining four sections, asking first what the team member listed as needs for performing better and ways they would like to experiment with improvements. Again, add only what you listed that might extend or add to what the team member mentions.

As you work through this creative work, keep a few best practices in mind. Ask your team member to:

Dig deeper

- Can you analyze the root causes of this issue?
- Can you see more opportunities to empower and develop yourself?

Avoid rescuing

- Allow silence. It is an opening for the other person to discover something themselves, to learn to go deeper.
- See the challenge as an invitation to new levels of self knowledge and self empowerment.

Clarify initiative and risk tolerance

- Clarify the level of initiative they can take.

- Increase their level of risk tolerance so they can make their own best decisions and keep moving autonomously more often.

Own lack of clarity of expectations

- Own any issues with lack of clarity of expectations.
- Ask for advice on how to be more clear.
- Do not take lack of clarity as an excuse. Say, "I will try to be more clear, but request any clarity you need early and often. Don't disappear for days, then offer 'lack of clarity' as the reason something wasn't done."

Consider fit

- Consider if they simply might not have the innate talents required to perform this role well in the timeframe required.
- Collaborate on how to build a ramp to a new role that's a better fit.

Using the Performance Wisdom Jig helps keep our discussion objective and creative, which will feed the rigor of our experiments.

Everything is an Experiment

If we are honest with ourselves, this is all an experiment. We as leaders are running experiments, too.

- Do you know exactly how to do your job successfully or are you running another experiment today based on everything you have learned to date?
- Are you experimenting with approaches to difficult conversations and more effective meetings?

We are scientists who forgot we are in a lab. Sometimes, we forget that life and work is a giant series of interlocking experiments we're running on ourselves and each other.

Let's become really good scientists. This will determine how good a leader we are. The more we can keep this in mind, the happier, freer, more compassionate, and more creatively clear and courageous we can be.

Designing Experiments

As you list all the MOCA variables you can think of, circle the three most impactful elements of your analysis by asking, "Which might give us the biggest performance improvement?"

I have noticed a tendency to ignore variables we assume are uncontrollable even if they might be the biggest drivers of better performance. For instance, if I assume I can have no effect on a person's wasting of time, I might set some tight deadlines for them. But, the assumption that I cannot help the person change their habits is a form of helplessness. This may be your own learned helplessness, which is no longer acceptable as a curious leader. Scientists don't give up when experiments don't work, they just get clearer, bolder and more creative in their next attempt.

As you review the possible experiments, notice the level of effort required for making changes in each of those variables. Depending on your employee's level of motivation and realistic capacity for change, choose the element that balances potential reward and level of effort involved. In the beginning, choose the item that requires less financial cost and more effort by the employee to test and develop the will and motivation of your team members. This lets you avoid enabling and over investing in people who need to either step up or step out.

Work together to design an experiment based on a hypothesis about the variable and how it works. For instance, the employee may want to try a more positive motivation like personal pride or learning a new skill rather than avoiding getting caught unprepared in a meeting. We'll dig more deeply into these sources of motivation in chapter seven.

You can use the Humane Leadership Lab Notebook to design and track your experiments. Find the Lab Notebook template on the Wisdom Jigs page of our website– it is simple and will help structure your learnings.

Timing and Tempo of Meetings

The Performance Wisdom Jig works best when it's the foundation for your regular one-on-one meetings with team members. In fact, I often use it to orient new staff members on their first day. Why not give them the structure they will work within and be evaluated upon from the start?

Over time, how often we use this wisdom jig with our team members depends on their level of performance and their developmental needs. Team members who are exceeding expectations can set the cadence of their own follow-up meetings given that they occur frequently enough to build momentum and allow the leader to provide feedback on progress to the rest of the organization. Because building momentum and visible results is the key to sustained performance improvement, most organizations require at least monthly progress reporting even for top performers.

Do top performers need to be working on performance improvement at all? Of course they do. Top performers are probably those who will enjoy this process most because they are habitually looking for ways to optimize their results. Plus, as a leader, you will be learning what's possible from your best people as they push forward– their levels of achievement, their best practices, and winning habits. The top performers are also the ones who set the leading edge of your culture, so it's important that they are visibly pursuing performance improvement along with everyone else

Team members actively improving their performance to reach baseline expectations or personal goals should evaluate themselves using the Performance Wisdom Jig weekly. They can host you weekly to review their lab notebooks and update on the progress of their experiments. These check-ins can be ten minutes long, but should be given more time if more support is required to help the team member build momentum and skills.

Probationary or developmental employees may need longer meetings more frequently depending on the severity of their situation. I have had employees who required multiple check-ins per day as they were very close to performance-based dismissal. This level of leadership is not sustainable but it allows us to ensure that we leave no stone unturned in pursuit of having our team members succeed. It also provides rich data to support decisions about continued employment or alternative roles. This level of investment also helps the rest of the team know that you, their leader, are committed to their success even in challenging moments.

Upon completing the Performance Wisdom Jig in a meeting, immediately schedule a follow-up meeting based on this cadence to review and refine your experiments. Send the invitation for the next meeting as soon as possible after the meeting as this is another form of intentional attention. Your acts of follow through are acts of generative care and fair strength. This creates a continuous tie to your next review of their work. There is no perceived gap in your leadership of their performance improvement if they can already see their next check in date.

Using this well-timed process of performance evaluation and experimentation, we can take clear steps toward our agreed-upon desired performance and outcomes. A team member's engagement, satisfaction, and productivity increase when they feel supported and aligned with their leadership in developing their ability to contribute to the company's mission.

Self Leadership: Uncomfortable Discoveries

As stated earlier, the Performance Wisdom Jig process identifies and eliminates many excuses. People will reveal most of their excuses for poor performance and, across your entire team, this will soon uncover almost every conceivable excuse. Tasks to eliminate these excuses become your leadership work.

Over time, you will possess a very powerful set of data that creates tremendous clarity for you and your team members. From that moment on, you will each face into the core realities of intentions, actions and the gap between the two.

With this extreme clarity, most people rise to the occasion, taking actions with motivation based on clear intentions. It's fairly rare for a person with this level of clarity to not perform well. But, all humans since the beginning of time have occasionally experienced a disconnect between their intentions and their actions. Elevating our powers of self leadership is the key to aligning our intentions and actions.

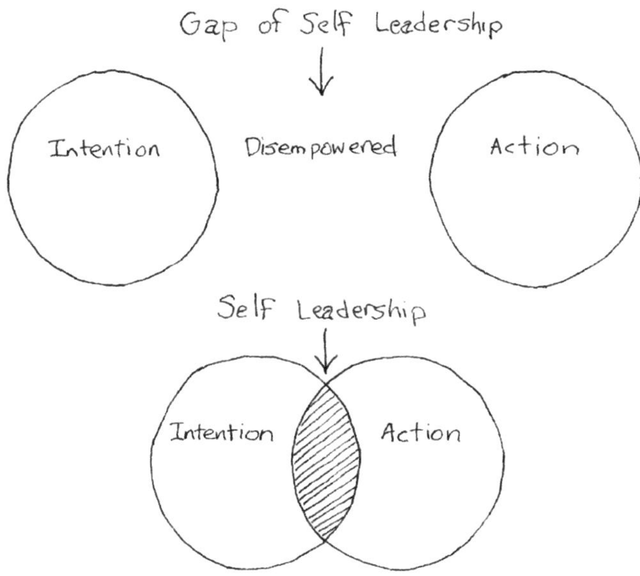

But, we must accept that some will not rise. As a leader who values performance, you want to know who will not rise as soon as possible. Front loading a new hire with the Performance Wisdom Jig model and a deliberate tempo of performance evaluation meetings will allow you to immediately design experiments to refine their ability to perform excellently– or not.

Of course, this chapter has been mostly about the happy path through performance improvement meetings. In the coming chapters, we will explore ways to work more deeply with each of the four variables and poke around in the murkier corners of human nature as we discuss the challenges we face as leaders.

Further Reading

- Dalio, *Principles,* 2017
- Descartes, *Rules for the Direction of the Mind,* 1637
- E.F. Schumacher, *A Guide For The Perplexed,* 1977
- Gehman, Interview on Intentional Attention with Humane Leadership website, 2018
- Huizinga, *Homo Ludens,* 1938
- Lencioni, *The Five Dysfunctions of a Team,* 2002
- O'Donohue, *Anam Cara,* 1996
- Sloan, Humane Leadership Lab Notebook, the HLC website

4

As you use the Performance Wisdom Jig, you may come up with some interesting questions:

- What is the leader's role in team performance?
- How do organizations create value and impacts?
- How are humane practices linked to impact?
- How does performance change?
- How can we reimagine organizations based on this?

These questions will support our performance improvement work by clarifying and shifting our approaches to change.

Reimagining Organizations and Work

To begin rethinking how we see organizations, let's fly up to 10,000 feet. From this height, we can imagine that organizations and the people in them look like forests full of trees. Each tree / person grows and provides some valuable resource, wood or fruit. The trees in a forest produce seeds, wood or shade, while humans gather to create goods (or services) like tamales for dinner, medical care for veterans, or avionic systems for hypersonic aircraft.

Now, if we fly down closer to the forest-organization, we will see that the trees are clustered and interacting, roots mingling, branches crossing. Richard Powers, in The Overstory, might even suggest the trees are working as a team. It's possible that the trees follow the cues of one tree more often to gain information and needed resources.

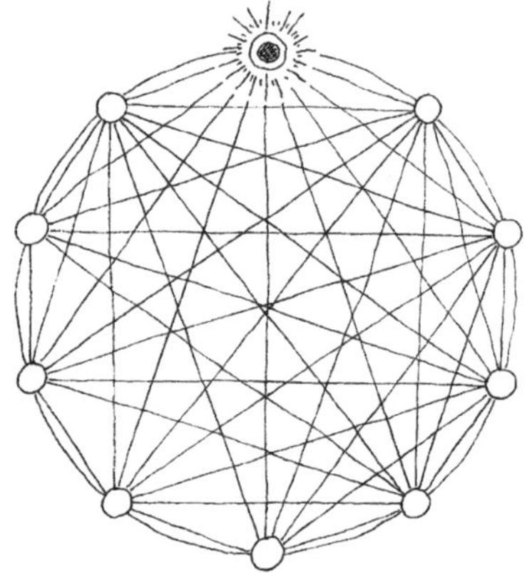

The leader's essential purpose is to help the individuals in the group reach shared goals more effectively. Any other agenda of a leader will soon inspire the team to choose a new leader to optimize their efforts.

Again, if we fly down even closer and look at the interactions between a leader and one other tree, we can see that their relationship can be categorized as either exploitative or edifying. It really is binary. In any one moment, we might be competing for resources or making space for each other to grow, either pursuing the interests of the group at the expense of investing in the growth of the individual tree or vice versa.

This dance can shift person to person and moment by moment, but, over time there will be a balance that characterizes the leader's relationship with the team as either mostly edifying or mostly exploitative.

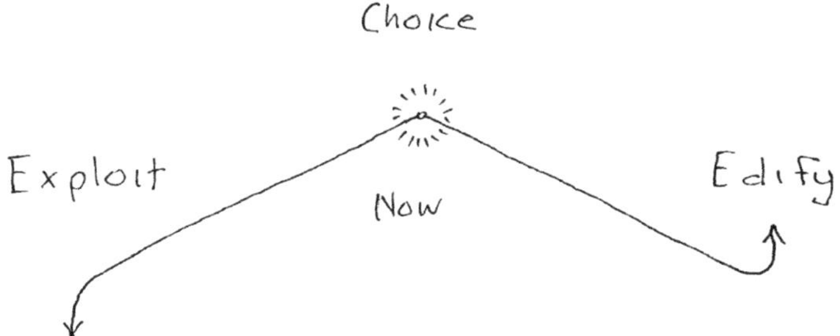

Of course, in both biological systems and human organizations, exploitation can have consolations or bribes built in. A business leader might think: "You do this uninteresting, compromising work for me and I will pay you for your time." A worker might think, "For this paycheck, I will give you my time, but I will not give you my heart and soul. I will just go through the motions, essentially disengaged." Every moment we work, we are dancing around these questions of exploitation and edification. I invite you to begin noticing this dance in and around yourself and your team.

Once we begin to notice this oscillation, the leader or the led can choose the path back towards edification. Even one additional question to clarify a shared goal or to better understand the other's desire for growth can shift the balance. These momentary choices are vitally important, because they accumulate into sources of hope and power or dismay and alienation.

The Leader's Role

A leader improves the performance of the people on their team. If they do not improve performance, they are an obstacle, not a leader. And the best leaders are chosen, not assigned.

Organizations may assign leadership roles, but real leaders earn the right to lead their teams. You can probably think of at least one leader in your organization who has the title, but often defers to the actual leader of the team who has earned the right to influence and improve the team's actions.

You can probably recall seeing a leader who has chosen the path of exploitation too often. Have you seen the parallel leadership structures quickly form around them, rendering them ineffective and, often, ridiculous?

Senior leaders and the human resources team can talk about culture, but team leaders create work culture moment by moment each day in their interactions with team members. The poster from HR might read, "There's no I in team," but one self-aggrandizing sentence from a team leader makes the poster irrelevant and even insulting in an instant.

Service Profit Chain: How Organizations Create Value

How does team culture and employee engagement and edification drive bottom line results?

We all seek to make a valuable difference to others. For some of us it's a social impact, for others it's a valuable commercial transaction. No matter the end value we seek to create, we all want to do that more effectively.

In the early 1990s, a group of academics met at the Harvard Business School and asked this question:

How do service organizations create value?

The service profit chain model emerged out of that small service management interest group's work. The group realized that satisfied, loyal, and productive employees were most effective at creating satisfied customers. In turn, satisfied customers increased bottom line profits by offering greater lifetime value and lowering sales costs.

The key links in the service profit chain from a humane leadership perspective are:

- **Moments of impact**– these are the touchpoints when your customers interact with your people, online presence and products and either experience wonder and joy, or not.
- **Employee engagement**– Leaders engage their team in creating moments of customer impact more effectively and more efficiently.
- **Virtuous cycle**– Leaders invest the profits earned from committed, long-term customers into developing next-level employee engagement and empowerment. These investment decisions by leadership reveal their commitment to customer satisfaction and humane leadership values.

The model has implications far beyond purely service organizations because every business has a service element; even heavy industry firms create customer satisfaction by having engaged, motivated, skilled employees delivering and installing their massive products.

The model has been put to profitable work by many leading organizations like Enterprise Rent-A-Car and Southwest Airlines. Enterprise even took the step of developing a measure to gauge customer experience outcomes that gained wide acceptance, the net promoter score ("How likely would you be to recommend us to a friend?").

Leaders working from the service profit chain model must focus their energy on their role in employee engagement. Unfortunately, in most organizations employee engagement is far below what we might hope or even imagine. Luckily, Gallup has been polling on this for years now and has some insights for us.

Employee Experience and Engagement

Over 30 years of research involving more than 25 million employees in 189 countries, Gallup has identified 12 elemental questions that powerfully link employee engagement to business outcomes by exploring employees' experience with supervisors and peers, clarity of expectations, and feedback focused on learning and development. For example, the survey includes questions like:

- In the last seven days have you received recognition or praise for doing good work?
- Is there someone at work who encourages your development?

- In the last year, have you had opportunities to learn and grow?

Much can be learned from Gallup's study. For instance, 70% of employee disengagement results from their direct leader's behaviors. Look at the questions above for clues as to what these levers might be (much more on this later). Gallup's findings show strong correlation between the positive answers to these questions, employee engagement and productivity.

Given the facts, our conversations about employee performance should be focused on the leader's performance. At the very least, leaders should enter performance conversations in a curious, collaborative frame of mind as we discussed in chapter three on performance improvement meetings. Let's start with this empowering assumption:

Humane leaders assume any team performance issue is rooted in a failure of leadership.

Our best employees are underperforming or leaving because of this failure of leadership. Gallup found that 50% of those surveyed had left a job at some point because of poor leadership. This statistic is telling only half the story; what about the workers who suffer under a poor leader and silently stay in your organization, underperforming?

Our best people are the first to leave a poor leader. So, it is possible that over time poor front line leadership will ensure that all your best people leave and your weakest players will stay on, disengaged and miserable. This puts our lack of productivity growth and our turnover in a new light.

Engagement is and must be held by front line leaders. Posters from HR and memos or videos from C-suite leaders are only window dressing compared to the power of the engaging communication, relationships, and professional development hosted by a team's front line leader.

In fact, engagement attempts from on high are actually destructive when poured over a poor leader's failings with their team. Team members are reminded how the organization's values are being subverted by their direct leader and how that subversion is being tolerated by top leadership. Possibly worst of all, workers may feel that their plight is invisible or irrelevant to those higher in the organization. Of course, disengagement and cynicism grow naturally in this wilderness.

Do you wonder what impact this unfortunate chain of events might be having on your organization's effectiveness today? We highly recommend you consider hiring Gallup to measure your team's engagement with their Q12 survey each year.

Clearly, engagement by front line leaders is important, but what role do managers play in the life of this wild organizational forest?

Managers Must Be Leaders

We believe that everyone who's not a direct producer is a leader and should be evaluated as one.

Your organization does not need managers, it needs effective leaders at every level. Managers maintain a status quo, leaders enable and empower what needs to emerge. This might seem like a flimsy distinction, but, in practice, leaders create the employee engagement, loyalty, and agility that drive the service profit chain's outcomes of profitability, growth, and impact.

This distinction between managers and leaders becomes crucial when we look at our desire for progress and our theories of change.

Progress and Your Theory of Change

Progress is change that moves us closer to our goals.

Leaders, by definition, assume that progress is possible and desirable. Great leaders engage their teams by showing them a path toward progress and helping them move deliberately forward on that path.

Unfortunately, many of those working on the leader's team don't believe that progress is a likely outcome. A talented, sharp young team might adore the idea of progress, but most workers are more "seasoned" and have learned by experience to temper their enthusiasm for what leaders presented in the past as "progress."

One day, working in a large company, I let out a deep sigh as I wrestled with data issues and the mind-boggling inertia of the organization. A long-time staffer in another department heard me and said, "Oh, the Bear Creek sigh! Don't worry, you'll get used to it."

Defiant, I said, "No, I never will. As soon as I can't make a difference here, I will leave." Admittedly that was not the greatest social move, but even in that stuck organization I insisted on making positive change and was soon moved into a series of leadership positions.

Leaders will always seek to drive positive change in themselves and in their team members. But how?

Whether we are conscious of it or not, we each work from a theory about how change unfolds. As mentioned in chapter one, our theories about how change happens in ourselves and in the outside world color our impressions and shape our actions.

Do you believe that if you give clear instructions and your people are "good" they will change their habits and reap the benefits? Have you ever been disappointed in this assumption?

Do you think that change only happens when we drive it with project management and strict accountability? "People respect what you inspect" or "If I can measure it, I can manage it."

Or maybe you lead by example. "If I work with tremendous energy and focus, the ducklings will follow. If they don't, I need new ducklings."

Maybe, you rely on the normal distribution curve of innovators, early adopters, the chasm, and early majority. You may find yourself wishing the laggards would get it already.

Each of these theories of change make assumptions about leaders, followers, and human nature that color our attitudes, approaches, and finally, our success. It is very important for you to be aware of your theory of change and to be curious about how it is working and how it might be upgraded. Your theory of change is crucial because it determines your ability to make progress. Of course, progress is the core of humane leadership and at the heart of two of Gandhi's three purposes of work: learning new ways to create value and transcending ourselves through collaboration.

A Humane Theory of Change

Our theory of change for individual performance is based on the biochemical mechanisms that shape our thoughts and actions. We think the most powerful place to create change is in the **sources** of thought and action, not in trying to compel action or to control thoughts directly.

Brain Chemistry

Think about your phone. Over the last several years, you have been trained by one app after another to seek surprise and delight through a new connection on LinkedIn, a fail on YouTube, or the very latest from friends on Snapchat. Usually, a little red number inspires us to click on the notification. Who replied? What am I missing?

App designers have used our addiction to the pleasure a dopamine release in our brains gives us to train us. Now, we hold our phones more closely than we hold our dearest humans. (Thanks, B.J. Fogg for teaching us about "conditioning technologies!" See the further reading section below for his contribution to using brain chemistry in user interface design.)

Given that dopamine loops naturally shape our behavior, humane leaders can create conditioning technologies of their own. We can modify behaviors by using more rewarding and empowering mental models, operating metaphors, and thought processes with our teams. Together, these create our humane leadership theory of change.

Models and Metaphors

To understand how this works, we build on the fact that what we call human experience is what we see, hear, etc. (sense data) structured by our mental models or operating metaphors (Lakoff).

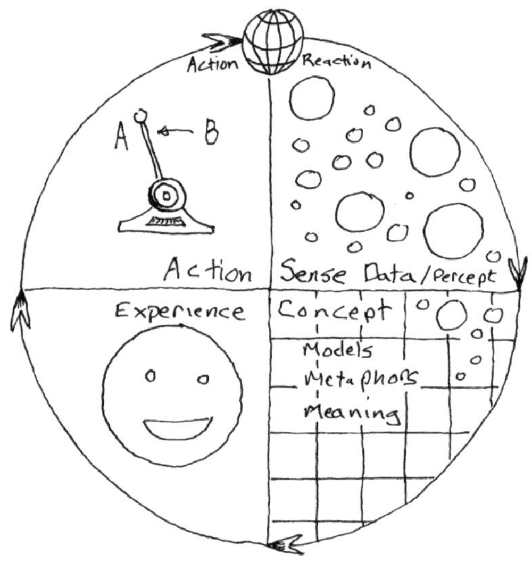

Turning sense data into experiences and actions

As you read this, the shape of contrasting black squiggles on white are being converted, via mental models and conceptual frameworks you and I share, into letters, words, sentences, and connected ideas in your mind. Your frameworks will create experiences of familiarity, confusion, or insight.

Imagine how confusing life would be if you had to categorize, name and evaluate the ideas of the letter S, smartphone, windows, tree, and sunlight afresh every time you encountered them? It is no wonder to me that babies are awake so little when they are first born, free of frameworks and all that uncategorized input to sort out!

A conceptual framework, or mental model, is a structure our minds use to organize information and our thinking. We start with Mama / not Mama, milk / not milk, but very quickly build all sorts of frames that help us sort out friends from threats, new from old, better from best and on and on until we are operating vehicles on highways, leading teams and comparing literature. In working life, when we hire people based on their education and experience we are actually hiring the mental models we hope they've developed.

We've adopted these models and metaphors from our social context, families, education, and work experience. For example, when a baby sees the interior of its home, it might have a simple, happy experience of nurturance. Holding the baby, looking at the same room, a mother might run her sense data through metaphors of nest, castle, or prison and mental models of family social structures, interior design, or mortgage finance, leaving her feeling safe, proud, or burdened.

Using mental models we can:

- Categorize sense data and ideas into usable information.
- Model relationships (correlation and causation).
    - For instance, distance = rate x time is a common mental model we use while traveling.

- Streamline our prioritization of inputs and facilitate thinking about what's most important right now.

Mental models:

- Can accumulate and become wisdom.
- Come to us subconsciously for the most part.
- Are only replaced when we find a clearly superior new model.
- Are created by humans and therefore can be refined and replaced at will.

Your new superpower is understanding the power of mental models and metaphors. Change your model, transform your experience and your performance.

If you think about a recent meeting in your organization, what metaphors did you use when discussing your organization's work and challenges? Were you tackling a project? Fighting fires? Mechanically converting inputs into outputs? Growing an ecosystem? Hitting home runs or picking low hanging fruit?

What was your experience of that meeting? Joyful collaboration? Stuck in a rut? On the verge of open conflict? Notice both the metaphor and your experience.

The first key to our theory of change is that changing our metaphors and the images they bring to mind will nearly instantly change our thinking, actions, and experiences.

What operating metaphor might be radically different from the one you habitually use, but relevant to your situation?

Now, think about your situation through a different operating metaphor.

To practice, invest a few minutes really thinking and learning about potential new metaphors for your situation:

- **Physics**: Do you gain any insight via the lenses of conservation of matter and energy? The second law of thermodynamics, entropy and reversion to the mean? The ideas of two objects not being able to occupy the same space at the same time, gravity, actions and reactions, or even quantum entanglement?
- **Permaculture**: How about the ideas of balanced, self-sustaining ecosystems? Production based on healthy soil and natural interactions between parts across daily, seasonal and lifespan timeframes? Human stewardship and nurturing of a variety of trees that grow and are fruitful in specific ways, like apple, plum and cherry trees?
- **Hospice care**: How about shifting the focus to care rather than solution or cure? To comfort and quality of life experience and connection in the limited time remaining? Maybe serving not only the patient or client, but their family and caregivers as well.

Which metaphors can you imagine offering new perspectives on your situation?

Time invested in approaching your situation through a new metaphor is both challenging and potentially transformational. Shifting our thinking sounds simple, but it is very hard for smart, successful humans to release the models and images that have, so far, rewarded them (Gribben). To try on the new metaphorical lens, ask yourself a few questions:

- What fits in the new model? What doesn't?
- Did the model shift my thinking and experience?
- Does this open new approaches to the challenge?
- What new possibilities and priorities emerged?

For instance, if you have been thinking of your team as a machine built of many components with specialized purposes bolted together, reimagining your team as a orchard will lead you to think of a team member as a:

- Naturally growing source of valuable fruit every year for 40 years or more.
- Living tree in your orchard, linked to all the others.
- Source of learning, inspiration and beauty.
- Sensitive indicator of the health of the soil and your skills as an orchardist.

Wisdom Jigs

The second element of our theory of change is based on thinking tools or wisdom jigs. To change our results we must change our actions. To change our actions, we must change our thoughts. To change our thoughts, we must give ourselves tools to help us internalize better ways of thinking. Recall

Buckminster Fuller's quote about how only tools can change the thinking of others in chapter one.

So, how do we operationalize models and habits of thought?

OODA Loops

I try to avoid military analogies in business, but sometimes they are really helpful. To guide fighter pilots in making urgent decisions in very difficult moments, US Air Force Colonel John Boyd created the OODA loop model.

The model holds that as we work at any task, we loop through four steps:

- Observe
- Orient
- Decide
- Act

As a fighter pilot, Boyd earned the nickname, Forty Second Boyd, because he could usually win a dogfight in under a minute by disorienting his adversary with a quick series of unexpected maneuvers. He defeated opponents by leaving them no time to complete their own OODA loops.

As we take the OODA loop steps in our somewhat more peaceful lives, we'll see that observing quickly and upgrading the mental models we use to orient ourselves will improve all our subsequent thoughts and actions. Just as Forty Second Boyd used a better model to win dogfights in the sky, business leaders need models to quickly turn data into insight and effective action every day. Even the mother and her baby are observing, orienting, deciding and acting based on constantly updated models and sense data. Let's explore how our theory of change integrates these ideas with an illustration.

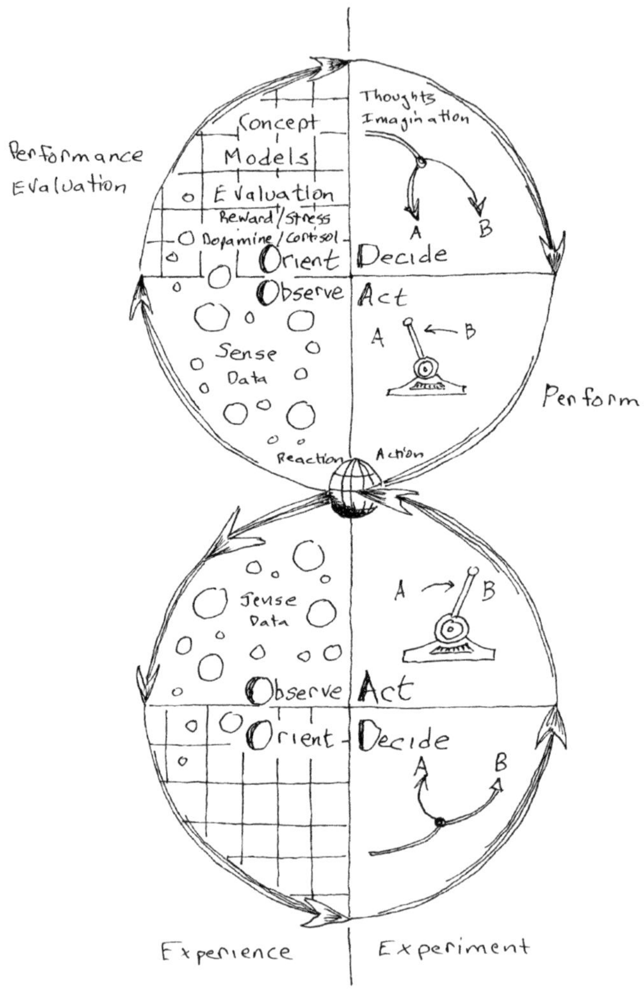

The humane performance leadership theory of change stack

The world offers a constant stream of sense data for us to **observe.** Starting at the center globe and moving up clockwise, our concepts, models and metaphors help us to filter, sort and find meaning in that data as we **orient** ourselves to it; dangerous / safe, image / word, useful / not. Concepts, metaphors and models give rise to images and thoughts. Thoughts are then evaluated and, eventually, we make **decisions** about right action. Decisions then become **actions** in the world at the center of the illustration, completing the first loop.

Then, transitioning down into the lower circle counter-clockwise, the world's reaction to our efforts creates new sense data and the lower OODA begins. After acting again, we return to the center.

Do the sense data and our mental models tell us our actions were successful? Let's do it again!

The anticipation of success releases **dopamine** in our brains, reinforces the actions we're taking (habits and addictive behaviors), and sends us off seeking more. Or, failure releases the stress hormone **cortisol** which causes us to avoid similar actions in the future. We loop infinitely between **experiences** in the world and **experiments** to improve our rewards and reduce our stress.

Humane leaders become conscious of and creative with the experiments they run. In this model, the variables at play are:

- **Data Sources**: How clearly, widely and deeply we observe the world.

- **Models**: How well-suited, complete we have made our set of conceptual models and operating metaphors that let us orient.
- **Thinking**: The rationality and clarity of our decisions.
- **Leadership**: The alignment and rapid linking of our intentions, decisions, and actions.

By refining these inputs, we can design our own dopamine loops to improve performance, engagement, and our experience of work (and life). As leaders become good at designing rewarding OODA loops that complete dopamine loops for themselves, they can begin to help others to design their own.

Performance review meetings quickly become design sessions around improving more effective, satisfying and edifying dopamine loops.

Dopamine loops of action and pleasure reinforce our new ways of thinking and acting. In a matter of a few weeks, our new mental models will be matched by very successful new habits in our behaviors. Thoughts, actions, performance, results and engagement all improve in a virtuous cycle.

For example, the writing of this book is the direct result of shifting my thinking about the process. I started out imagining the book as a critical project requiring discipline, focus and time I did not have. Early on, I observed that my approach was not working. So, I dug into my mindset around it and my deeper sources of motivation and reoriented myself by seeing the book as my path to freedom. Using that mental model, I picked up some radically productive new habits of thought and action and am more satisfied, inspired and energized in my writing.

The OODA loop is the basic structure of our self-leadership experiments. We each have everything we need to learn about improving the performance of humans in our private self leadership laboratories.

Every day can be a new experiment to refine your sources of motivation, your relationships to time and authority, the clarity of your planning, as well as the skills, tools and self development methods you use. Everyone has a self leadership lab, but most of us could become much more creative and conscientious scientists.

So, our theory of change hinges on consciously choosing to experiment with more useful, engaging data sources and mental models to build reward loops that will deliver progress for ourselves, our teams and organizations.

Whole Or Part?

An important question remains:

Where does change actually happen?

Does change happen in the organization and influence the people in it? Or, does change happen in the individuals who make up the organization? We believe that each transformed individual shifts the center of habitual and cultural gravity of the organization.

We believe that the unit of change is the individual and that the health of the team or organization is simply the sum of the health of the individuals in it. Healthy growing parts make up a healthy, growing whole.

Imagining an organization as an intricately woven set of individuals acting as parts of an ecosystem allows us to apply systems thinking approaches to organizational development. Thinking about how systems emerge, function and evolve maps very usefully to thinking about organizations of complex adaptive systems (humans) working in complex adaptive systems (organizations, industries, and markets). There's a lot of good material available on systems thinking (Senge), so we'll now turn our attention to the powerful levers for change at the individual level.

Leadership, Opportunity and Performance

Humane leadership reveals itself in how we hold individual people in relationship to their performance, opportunities, and personal potential.

A leader's job is to create good opportunities and connect people with them, just as a teacher will recommend a book to open new perspectives for a student, a swim coach will ask an athlete to try swimming a longer race than usual, and a business leader will offer a challenging new project as an opportunity to stretch, learn, and contribute. Leaders set out opportunities for growth and flow that Csikszentmihalyi describe as not passive or relaxing, but moments when "a person's body or mind is stretched to its limits in a voluntary effort to accomplish something difficult and worthwhile."

A humane leader often has more faith in the team members than they have in themselves, while less effective leaders often impose their own limits and fears onto others. Humane leaders see what we can become and offer us challenging, nurturing opportunities and space to grow to our full potential.

Think back. Years ago, one of your best teachers or coaches probably saw something in you and said, "I think you can be better than you realize." You stepped into that possibility and you likely found out it was true. The mentor's vision and faith helped you reach your current level in life.

The Dark Side of Humans

Humane leaders hold faith in each human's potential even in the darkest moments, especially in the darkest moments. Rather than avoid the hard moments, humane leaders step in and engage as soon as appropriate. Once a situation has settled down, the leader might say, "Let's look clearly at what's going on, and look positively at what we can do about it." So, a very focused and potentially productive performance improvement conversation begins.

Our theory of change includes the acceptance of the needs and potentials of all the humans (workers and leaders) involved in the process; not just their mental or emotional states, but also their physical and even moral / spiritual states.

Rather than avoid doubts, fears, and physical needs, we seek to learn from them to maximize actual rather than idealized performance. In an ideal world, we'd all charge out of bed, give it 120% all day, and sleep like babies each night. Alas, few of us live like that. We live in the dark soil of our own humanity.

Luckily, hidden in those dark depths are the unseen sources of our growth.

Humane leaders acknowledge that:

- Hard things happen.
- Most humans have a strong "I don't want to" element in our personalities.
- We get really frustrated and can be paralyzed by perfectionism.
- We often fall short of what we know is better behavior.
- Discouragement, sadness and anxiety sometimes overtake us.

At the same time, humane leaders will hold the possibility of something beyond present challenges by saying, "This is today's reality, but it doesn't have to be tomorrow's. What can we try next?"

Humane leaders hold the person and their potential in close relationship over time so the person can unfold toward their full potential.

Humane leaders hold hope and faith earlier and longer than anyone else, using conceptual frameworks that create an inspiring, humane vision of improved performance and change. This is how people are engaged, teams are built, and performance is improved in an organic, sustainable, profitable way.

Further reading

- Csikszentmihalyi, *Flow: The Psychology of Optimal Experience,* 1990
- Fogg, *Persuasive Technology,* 2002
- Gribben, *Ice Age: A Theory That Came In From the Cold,* 2001
- Lakoff & Johnson, *Metaphors We Live By,* 1980
- Sasser, et al, "Putting the Service Profit Chain to Work," Harvard Business Review, 1994
- Senge, *The Fifth Discipline: The Art & Practice of The Learning Organization,* 1990

5

Edges Define the Middle

New theoretical models and idealized processes are fun, but really good, humane leaders are defined by how they handle the exceptions, the really tough edge cases. While we hope to be known for our good days and soft interiors, too often it's our crackly, brittle exterior in moments of challenge that defines our reputation as a leader.

Is it true that anything really meaningful in life (love, heroism, beauty, leadership) must be glimpsed as a series of impressions at the edges of the action rather than described directly? As in poetry, do the details at the edges gradually reveal the heart and meaning of the idea?

Similarly, the beauty of an island can only really be imagined by describing its edges, how it looms up from a sparkling sea dotted with islets, how its cliffs, gray against the white morning sky, are fringed with the deep green of native herbs and the bright pink-purple of bougainvillea that climbs its white homes, clustered in the protected vales atop the cliffs.

Less appealingly, your leadership will be defined by how you handle your own biases, the extremes, the edge cases, the difficult people and situations you and your team face.

Unless we are aware of the distortions in our own lens we won't be able to see other's challenges clearly. Or, as a wise man once said, "Remove the log from your own eye before trying to remove the speck of dust in someone else's."

The Leader's Own Edges

We want to be aware, not perfect. Our goal is self knowledge. Aspiring to be a humane leader frees us from the need to strive for perfection. We can simply try to avoid the big errors and good things will begin to happen. So what are the big errors at the edges of our own humanity?

In this chapter, we'll start with the most innocent edges and errors and words towards the darker challenges we might bring to the performance improvement table.

Edge 1: Distraction

Our first and most common error is forgetting to be present with ourselves and others. Modern work environments, with lots of people and technology packed into open working spaces, are almost designed to distract us. Workers desperate

Oversized helmet eliminates noise, dignity.
h/t Geek.com

to be productive have gone to great (ridiculous) lengths to overcome the challenges of distraction.

This edge starts with a growing wilderness of communications channels on our many devices. But the demands of others on our attention is not new. In the year 1820, Thomas Jefferson, in his retirement, told John Adams that he "suffered under the persecution of letters [1,267 per year]... many of them requiring answers of elaborate research, and all to be answered with due attention and consideration." All the data and queries coming at us distract us when we're with another person or our own thoughts, then they accumulate into huge piles of unread emails, notifications and other inputs that pull us away from our own values, plans and work.

Another dangerous form of distraction is the shiny new object (idea, expert, opportunity) that pulls us away from the long obedience required to nurture our own clear, creative thinking and well-laid plans. Authority bias can distract us from the wisdom available within our own organizations. How often do you let new ideas from outside your organization distract you from completing a perfectly good homegrown plan or experiment?

If we love wisdom, we will seek it everywhere; from everyone and everything we encounter. In our efforts to escape disruption and myopia, we must be cautious to avoid the brilliant idiots, the ones who are articulate, informed, credentialed, persuasive and wrong. Ray Dalio explains a variety of methods his firm uses to avoid being distracted by brilliant idiots in his book, *Principles*.

Mindfully curating our own consciousness is a foundation of humane self leadership. Those who successfully learn to curate their consciousness will become important leaders to those who have been swept along with the distracting tides of our culture. One useful indicator of successful curation might be hours of reading, analyzing, and synthesizing to support your strategic goals versus hours consuming news, games, and entertainment (Postman).

The path forward to avoid distraction is to practice giving the gift of intentional attention to yourself and to others throughout your day, not just while you sit in meditation (Gehman). From this intentional awareness, you can better curate your consciousness, set boundaries, and minimize wasting your time on other people's priorities.

Edge 2: Lack of Self Examination

> The unexamined life is not worth living.
>
> — Socrates in Plato's *Apology*

Leadership calls for a search for truth and ongoing refinement of goals and approaches. Leaders must dig relentlessly for root causes and higher purposes.

A useful way to understand our challenges is root cause analysis. To find a root cause of your distraction, you might ask a series of deepening "whys:"

Q: Why was I distracted?
A: My phone rang.

Q: Why did your phone ring?
A: Because it was on my desk and I had my ringer on.

Q: Why was your ringer on and your phone on your desk?
A: I forgot to turn my ringer off before I met with Darlene and I was afraid I would miss that critical call from client B.

Q: Why did you forget to turn your ringer off?
A: I was running in from my last meeting.

Q: Why were you afraid of missing the call from client B?
A: No one else is capable of handling this deal; it's too big and important.

Q: Why were you running late from your prior meeting?
A: I am over promising by not scheduling myself with realistic travel times between meetings.

Q: Why can't anyone but you handle this client?
A: I overpromised rather than clearly offering only what the team can easily do.

Q: Why am I over promising?
A: I am afraid that what I do, who I am, is not good enough to succeed.

Q: Why do you lack confidence?
A: Because I have overpromised in the past and failed to deliver.

Q: What can I do to prove my worth to myself?
A: Schedule myself with ample time to move between meetings and prepare to be really present with people. Preplan what we can offer and deliver well. Only offer what is on the plan no matter how hopeful or insecure I am feeling in the moment.

This process is very simple and methodical, but it can lead to very impactful questions and experiments. If the leader in the example above investigates the insecurities that lead to over-promising and experiments with avoiding making promises the team cannot easily meet, imagine how everyone's experience and ability to contribute might be transformed, not to mention, how much more present the leader might be with his team and clients going forward.

> It's extraordinary how we go through life with eyes half shut, with dull ears, with dormant thoughts. ... [But most of us have]... known one of these rare moments of awakening when we see, hear, understand ever so much– everything– in a flash– before we fall back again into our agreeable somnolence.
>
> — Joseph Conrad, *Lord Jim*

Of course, we have a wisdom jig on our website to support your search for root causes and deeper insight, the Root Cause Analysis Wisdom Jig.

Edge 3: Mechanism

We often make the error of reverting to a formulaic approach to our work. We hide behind roles, rules, and processes to avoid engaging with people and opportunities that are likely to get messy. We often feel compelled to behave mechanically because we feel hopelessly disempowered in our positions. Beware if you find yourself saying, "I wish I could, but..." or "Our policy is..." or "I don't make the rules, but..."

Hopeless disempowerment is a temporary condition that requires decisive corrective action. We must find the variables we can control and experiment with them to realign our intentions and actions so that we regain our agency, our self leadership. If we cannot find power and hope within the current organization, we must look beyond it to find a situation that will provide opportunities to live, try, and contribute.

Edge 4: Anxiety

Lack of courage and faith can undermine our effectiveness by causing us to obsessively collect feedback, market data, second opinions, more data, more measures, more often, dashboard, deeper analyses, and wow, machine learning!

Obsession with magic bullets, real-time data, and new consultants will drive you and others crazy. This endless second guessing and pursuit of justification rather than making courageous decisions based in clear thinking is tiring and depressing to everyone involved. These fearful habits destroy hope and motivation by delaying action and distracting from plans designed and agreed by the team.

Opportunity and motivation are both fast-fading flowers. Humane leaders see the bud before it blooms and they enjoy the flowering before it fades. Courageous leaders are alchemists who turn worry into the focused energy required to collect the best data, make clear decisions and act, now.

GK Chesterton, writing about Charles Dickens, said,

> Not only did his life necessitate work, but his character necessitated worry about work; and that combination is always one which is very dangerous to the temperament which is exposed to it. The only people who ought to be allowed to work are the people who are able to shirk. The only people who ought to be

> allowed to worry are the people who have nothing to worry about. When the two are combined, as they were in Dickens, you are very likely to have at least one collapse.

Can you shirk, keeping life and work in wise balance and healthy perspective? Do you worry without focusing your energy on action? In what ways is this affecting your ability to lead yourself and your team? Is collapse imminent or just likely at some point? What might you change to avoid it?

One key change is to maintain a healthy perspective on work and stop thinking it's terribly important. We would be wise to remember that before we were here, the world functioned just fine and will continue without us. For now, we can make life a bit better, easier, or nicer for others.

With this perspective, it becomes important to think only when there's a good reason to do so; new data, a new model, or a required decision. Mindfully disciplining and focusing our thinking yields focus, courage, and peace.

> To conquer fear is the beginning of wisdom.
>
> — Russell, *The Conquest of Happiness*

Edge 5: Lack of Care

Even in the West, we can fall into caste thinking based on our ideas of talent, hard work, and superiority. In a culture that idolizes success, we tend to heap attention, resources, and opportunities upon the stars, the winners, and the leaders of the pack, while faulting those who haven't attained high status as lazy, lesser, or lacking in ability.

Some may think that maintaining their status requires that they keep others at arm's length, as does the recently wealthy, stuffy Dickens character Mr. Dorrit, who said,

> No, it is incumbent upon all people in an exalted position,... to make themselves respected. To be vigilant in making themselves respected. Dependents, to respect us, must be– ha– kept at a distance and– hum– kept down. Down.

While this may seem abhorrent and archaic, I bet you can recall seeing people behaving this way in your own life experience– and getting promoted.

Science does not back up our tendency to invest more in "winners." A study by Italian physicists (Pluchino and Raspisarda) and economist (Biondo) on the role of luck in success found that our current focus on winners is a:

> "naive meritocracy," which fails to give honors and rewards to the most competent people, because it underestimates the role of randomness among the determinants of success.

For a moving and generous novel-length exploration of the role of luck in success and failure, I heartily recommend Charles Dickens' *Little Dorrit* of 1857.

What can you do about this leadership challenge? First, consider differences of "success so far:" values, approach, luck, privilege, and ability. Your skills and qualities may have won you a position in the social experiment (organization or profession) you are in now, but they will not always help you win going forward. So, with the people on your team, be humble, present, engaged, and creative in pursuit of their best opportunities to win going forward.

A leader's stewardship of opportunities is key to her success. When Google studied the qualities of their best managers in their Project Oxygen, they analyzed a huge amount of data about manager and team performance and found that opening opportunities for their team members' professional growth was a key driver of manager success.

Humane leaders care deeply for their team. They dedicate themselves to engaging the humans on their team with humble curiosity, empathy, compassion around needs, and careful nurturing of skills, habits, and opportunities for growth. This book supports the development of all of these humane leadership skills.

Edge 6: Lack of Prudence

The quality of our thinking determines the quality of our decisions, which helps determine our outcomes.

Prudent

1. *Acting with or showing care and thought for the future. Synonyms: Wisdom, judgment, sagacity.*

A lot of leadership errors can be avoided by addressing our under-developed critical thinking skills. We keep falling into well known cognitive biases and logical fallacies, as well as using data and rationalization to justify whatever we feel like doing.

> Vanity plays lurid tricks with our memory, and the truth of every passion wants some pretence to make it live.
>
> — Joseph Conrad, *Lord Jim*

As Amazon's 13 Leadership Principles point out, "Leaders are right, a lot." It is imperative for leaders to work diligently over their lifetimes to improve their ability to think clearly and understand what's true (Parrish). Much more on this in chapters ten and eleven, but a few powerful, detailed accounts of seeking to think more clearly and live more consciously include Descartes' *Discourse on Method*, Thoreau's *Walden*, and David Whyte's *The Heart Aroused*.

Edge 7: Breaking Trust

Leaders depend on the trust of their team, but trust is slowly built and easily damaged.

Employees trust us to make and keep basic promises around pay and benefits, but they also trust us to:

- Grow opportunities for them and their teammates.
- Create visions and follow plans.
- Be fair in the distribution of opportunities and rewards.

- Create transparency around collective deliberation.
- Exercise prudence in decision making.
- Execute plans diligently.

Stumbles in any one of these leadership functions will damage our team's faith in us.

Working towards greater consciousness of the promises we are making tacitly or directly will make us more solid and more inspiring leaders. Though easily stated and read, this is a lifetime's work for most humans.

What promises are you struggling to keep?

Don't worry, it's not just you, this has been a problem since the couple in the garden saw a snake in a fruit tree. The question is: How will you relate to this reality today? Give up, whip yourself, become self righteous? Or, will you become more conscious and begin experimenting with new ways of holding your integrity by promising more carefully and investing more in keeping your promises?

Edge 8: Self Absorption

Often hiring and promotion practices seem to reward narcissistic and sociopathic behavior. The person with charm, cunning, and fearless calm under pressure is often rewarded with leadership positions. These people can be excellent in times of crisis, but can do great damage in the times that call for more collaborative, nurturing approaches. Really great humane leaders can adapt to what each situation requires without compromising their values.

But, even the most socially adapted leaders can be pushed into a state of self absorption by overwhelming circumstances or the experience of power itself.

Sometimes the circumstances leaders find themselves in push them to prioritize their own needs over those of the team. One of Napoleon's aides describes a moment in September of 1812 as Moscow burned and French army leaders rested in a wooden building, hot ashes falling on the roof. When the winds suddenly changed, one of the officers rolled over to fall back to sleep, saying that now it was someone else's problem.

> For such was the callousness engendered by this onslaught of events and misfortunes, such the selfishness born of fatigue and suffering, that each one of us had retained only the measure of feeling and strength necessary for his service and personal preservation.
>
> — De Ségur

Humane leaders work hard to apply reasonable foresight to avoid putting themselves and others into such dire situations. Unfortunately for hundreds of thousands of French and Russian soldiers, Napoleon rushed maniacally toward a terrible fate, exhausting his own (and others') reason and compassion.

It is possible that he fell prey to the fact that the experience of power corrupts many of us by encouraging our self absorption?

Berkeley's Dacher Keltner writes of a "power paradox:" that the best in human nature earns us power, but the mushy or sharp edges of our character create the conditions for our fall from influence.

> We gain a capacity to make a difference in the world by enhancing the lives of others, but the very experience of having power and privilege leads us to behave, in our worst moments, like impulsive, out-of-control sociopaths.

Power brings our latent moral and spiritual challenges to the surface. It's almost like leadership roles hold up a bright light and a mirror to the realities of our own character. We might wrap our love of power and habits of self absorption in the flags of greatness or commitment to the grand vision, but in the end, we are simply exposing and exorcising our own challenges in public.

Leaders may not actually be corrupted, just self-absorbed, prioritizing their own needs and desires over those of the team. Either way, it's an edge that can damage our ability to lead.

By nature or habit, some leaders are selfishly drawn to the heroic opportunities and thrills commanding in a crisis creates. Their minds find calm clarity in the moment of greatest challenge. A few days ago, I was talking to a fire captain who sheepishly lamented that last summer he didn't have any major wildfires to fight. He felt aimless and wistful without the intoxicating clarity of a crisis.

Leaders who thrive on adrenaline will create crises to fulfill this, often subconscious, need. As a leader who enjoys feeling heroic, I try to exercise wise balance and avoid creating chaos or bold new initiatives just to create intense experiences. Sadly, many leaders, some being my dear clients, drag themselves, their teams and their families from one huge, draining adventure to the next.

Some moments of crisis call for steely determination, but our culture has permitted this mode of crisis leadership to infect many teams' daily interactions with stretch goals, forcing functions and aggressive accountability. As leaders, self awareness, nurturance of others, and collaborative experiments with alternative approaches are our best hopes for avoiding bringing this pollution into our team's work.

Edge 9: Cynicism

Leaders who have lost faith in their team, their organization, and maybe even themselves inflict the most damage.

Cynicism reveals our lack of hope that doing what's right is a viable path forward. Cynicism leads us to undermine our own right to lead other humans by justifying exploitation and abuse. In extreme cases it may blind us to the impact of our actions, like laying off several long-term employees to cut costs one afternoon then showing up in a new Porsche the next morning (true story, not me!)

Often, the more experience we gain, the more evidence we have to justify our cynicism– our own and other people's inability to consistently do the right thing, the promotion of people with sociopathic tendencies, fame and fortune being showered on undeserving others, and the moral compromise built into many large scale endeavors. There are many perfectly good reasons to be cynical; unfortunately, cynicism will kill us, our teams, and our organizations.

In the face of my own growing cynicism, I learned that

> The antidote to cynicism is impeccability.

A person who can be trusted with little will be trusted with much. Being impeccable with our values, honesty and responsibilities will lead us away from cynicism. Even though it's not convenient, our privileges carry obligations. With freedom and power comes responsibility.

If we look outside of ourselves, we can be convinced that we can get away with shortcuts, but if we look within, we realize that only the narrow road of responsibility leads us to become the type of human we aspire to be.

> Integrity is doing the right thing even when no one is watching.
>
> — C. S. Lewis

Not all leaders seek integrity. I am reminded of a modern leader's statement, "when you're a star, they let you do it. You can do anything." That is a pure example of teleological thinking; the ends justifying the means. If "they let you" does not make "it" right.

The deeper question is, who are you seeking to be in this life?

You didn't aspire to be cynical. Did you allow life to "make" you cynical? Can you return to living from your highest values?

To chart your course away from cynicism, start with the humane leadership values. See how you might allow yourself to think and act out of those values a bit more frequently today. That will start your journey back.

Or, know that the power of leadership is like being handed a good, strong rope and freedom to use it. In my experience, working from fair strength, generative care and wise balance help us avoid a sudden snug feeling around our necks.

As leaders we hold people's hope and faith in our hands. Our thoughts lead to actions which have consequences for everyone around us. So, when we choose to think and act cynically, we are undermining the hope and faith of everyone around us.

Impeccable integrity lets you become the leader others need. Your final exam begins now and lasts the rest of your life.

This may make you not want to lead at all. Unfortunately, it's too late for that. You are already leading yourself and, by example, everyone around you no matter your role or age. Unfortunately, you cannot unread this. The virus of integrity has infected you. Your path forward has been altered even if you immediately burn this book. Sorry, and you're welcome.

Promises and The One Inch Puddle

Given all of this, what can we do?

We can start by getting humble and real. Look closely at the scope of your current work. Is the light of your good character shining purely through all of your responsibilities?

> The moon is reflected even in a puddle an inch wide.
>
> — Dogen

Our minds can sign up for vast challenges. But have we taken responsibility for a puddle so big that we cannot help but be cynical about all that's reflected in it? Have our responsibilities overwhelmed our ability to shine purely and impeccably through? Are we staggering emotionally, physically, or morally under the load we've taken on?

How can we start redefining the limits of our responsibility? Maybe start with Shakespeare's wisdom in Hamlet,"To thine own self be true."

- What can you do in your current role that's aligned with who you aspire to be, the light you hope to reflect into the world?
- Is the unmanageable scope of your current responsibilities causing you to become imbalanced and cynical?
- What could you hand off to start your journey back toward personal integrity?

Being the person who carefully makes and keeps promises might be the ultimate way of being true to yourself.

What are organizations other than promise-making and keeping organisms made up of individuals doing the same?

- You give me five dollars, I will hand you a sandwich.
- You send us your students and we will help them become functional young adults.
- You send us your payload and we'll put it into orbit.
- Work here and we'll give you purpose and pay.

Successful organizations make and keep a lot of promises every day. Of course, some promises are bigger than transactions. Being true to our shared values and to our own integrity are the foundational promises we must keep.

One of the promises we can make to ourselves is to work in organizations aligned with our own values, because we are each implicated in the actions of the organizations we join.

I was consulting recently and it suddenly became clear to me that the client was moving off the agreed plan for scaling operations and heading in a direction that did not align with my values. I had a moment of real despair. How was I going to avoid implication and cynicism now?

Seconds later, a worker came up to me and said that some metal shavings had gotten into his eye as he drove a forklift. I was consulting in organizational development, process and system engineering, but I knew he saw me as a leader. A supervisor suggested the worker walk a few blocks to an urgent care facility.

In that moment, I saw a choice between cynicism and impeccability. I saw that above my huge and pressing tasklist, I could be the person who lived our shared company values of CARE (Connect, Achieve, Respect and Emerge).

So, I led the man to my car and drove him to urgent care. I stayed with him for the next few hours as he worked his way through layers of specialists and medical offices to clean out his eye and ensure he would have no lasting damage. In the process of being with him that afternoon, I was able to connect with him as a human being across the divides of role, education, and life experience that separated us.

This experience gave me the power to remain in my integrity, gave the entire organization an experience of what caring leadership looked like, and connected me to one more human being who later became an important ally. I was lucky to be free to choose impeccability. Soon afterwards, I ended my contract with that organization because of our misaligned values and immediately started writing this book.

Once we are true to your highest aspirations for being, we may choose to focus on impeccably holding our team members within a larger, more callous organization. This may not shift the values of the organization in the short term, but you can hold your own values within your team. As you do, you will begin looking for ways to either change the organization from within or change which organization you work in.

> Tell me what company you work for and I will tell you what kind of human you are.
>
> — Emmanuelle Duez at 2018 Global Peter Drucker Forum

Organizations may reward obsession with customers, mission, growth, or profits, but as they plow forward we as individuals cannot help but be implicated in the moral, social and environmental compromises they make.

How much can you hold impeccably?

Is your organization supporting your impeccability?

Know Thyself

How can we honestly, effectively address these challenges and opportunities?

In the entry court of the Oracle at Delphi was the inscription,

> Know thyself.

Socrates credits the inscription for a key to his wisdom which he later described by saying,

> What I do not know, I do not think I know.

Humble self knowledge will help us with the challenges at the edges of our work with our teams.

Thoreau, in *Walden*, sets the context nicely for our next adventure:

> Actually, the laboring man has not leisure for a true integrity day by day. ...He has no time to be anything but a machine. How can he remember well his ignorance– which his growth requires– who has so often to use his knowledge? ...The finest qualities of our nature, like the bloom on fruits, can be preserved only

> by the most delicate handling. Yet we do not treat ourselves nor one another thus tenderly.

May we each slow down the machines of our work to find a more tender path. This may allow us to be impeccable with our chosen puddles of responsibility. The clarity and integrity we reflect will be a great gift to ourselves and our world.

Further Reading

- Conrad, *Lord Jim*, 1900
- Dalio, *Principles*, 2017
- Descartes, *Discourse on the Method of Rightly Conducting One's Reason and of Seeking Truth in the Sciences*, 1637
- De Ségur, *Defeat: Napoleon's Russian Campaign*, 2008
- Dickens, *Little Dorrit*, 1857
- Gehman, Interview on Intentional Attention with Humane Leadership Institute, 2018, humaneleadershipinstitute.org
- Keltner, *The Power Paradox: How We Gain and Lose Influence*, 2016
- Parrish, Farnam Street Blog
- Pluchino, Raspisarda, Biondo, *Talent vs Luck: The Role of Randomness in Success and Failure*, 2018
- Postman, *Amusing Ourselves to Death*, 1985
- Thoreau, *Walden, Or, Life in the Woods*, 1854
- Whyte, *The Heart Aroused*, 1994

6

The Edges of Your Team

We're already curious about our own challenges, many of which our teammates will share. Now we extend our curiosity to our teammates.

We can see the reality of their performance and the variables that are driving it as clearly as possible. How we handle these challenging edge cases will, again, determine the quality of our leadership.

To support your humane leadership, we've built this chapter as a reference to use in moments of challenge.

We've addressed each challenging situation, each edge, with a quick overview, and we've built a set of tools to support your curious, clear, constructive approach:

Curious

- Telltale signs of the challenge
- Questions to support your curiosity about it

Clear

- Questions to clarify the edge and its impacts on performance and the team.
- Identify which P(MOCA) variables might be creating the edge.

Constructive

- Questions to help you collaborate to discover mental models that may need upgrading and to develop experiments to overcome the challenge.

We've arranged the edges so that levels of team member honesty and virtue decrease as we move down the list from the honestly confused toward the darkly cynical. The numbering of these edges builds from the prior chapter because we all face these challenges over time.

As you work through these edges with your team members, you will discover which variables of P(MOCA) are at work. This is an extremely important step for you as leader to complete with your team members in performance improvement meetings. The following four chapters will explore each variable in depth, offering mental models, wisdom jigs, and other approaches to improving performance.

Edge 10: Overwhelm and the Fog of Work

Business begets busyness.

A growing, thriving enterprise creates a lot of conversation, work, and data. This, together with modern open offices, global business and a multiplicity of communication channels, creates a lot of distraction and fog.

Our workers are subject to distraction by all of this chatter and chaff. It seems our work environments were designed to break our OODA loops by taking away their time to observe, orient, decide and act. This is a major challenge for leaders in every age, creating and maintaining clarity of expectations around focus, method and priority.

Signs of the Fog of Work challenge. A team member says:

- "I did this, but it might not be what you needed done."
- "I didn't know…" Pleading ignorance despite having task lists, checklists and standard operating procedures.
- "Tell me what you want, how you want it and when you want it."
- "I was waiting for instructions or permission."
- "I needed a decision."
- "I was scrambling and I forgot."

Curious– as leader, you can ask:

- "What did you think the expectation was?"

- "Were unclear or conflicting expectations communicated?" then, "Let's see what's in the instructions, the project plan, your notes, etc."
- "How can you (the team member) help the team clarify expectations before starting work?"
- "Were you clear to start with, then lost clarity over time?"
- "Do you have a daily checklist or project plan to help you return to clarity each day?"

Clear– as leader, you can:

- Review their prioritized task list, project plan and/or daily checklist
- Ask, "Do we need to refine our project planning and leadership processes and skills?"
- "How might your lack of clarity create challenges for our teammates and clients?"
- "Whose responsibility is it to maintain your clarity?"

Constructive

- "How can you ensure your own clarity each day?" This should be efficient, methodical and non-intrusive to others on the team.
- "Taking notes on your promises and opportunities to earn influence is a required skill and habit here." Review their notes and offer suggestions at the end of each meeting until their note-taking skills and habits are well established.

- "Proactively block out time to keep the promises you've made." Review their calendar habits to support their placement of work in time.
- Using Agile or another project/teamwork coordination methods (more on this in chapter eight).
- Develop daily checklists for each role. The team member can create the first draft that you can refine collaboratively over time.
- Reducing channels of communication and instituting need-to-know practices around including people in conversations that don't directly affect their work. Don't wantonly cc people just to be nice– give them peace until their input is required. Think of work as a relay race, not a scrum.
- "How do you triage your communications?" Support the development of sophisticated approaches to managing email and other communications channels. There's a lot of good advice available online.

As leaders, we can build or destroy clarity for our teams. Sometimes what we think are great ideas and exciting new opportunities might be inadvertently creating fog. Ask your team how you might help adjust your own habits to clear the fog.

Edge 11: Inert Good Intentions

We may want to perform well, but we may not do what's necessary to actually improve our results.

Signs of the Inert Good Intentions challenge:

- Agreeable, sociable person who's slowing down the team, lagging or not actively working to improve results.
- Seeking to connect and please; warm, friendly and communicative, but lax with deliverables and loose on targets and timing.
- Ability shortfalls without diligent self-development.
- Lack of disciplined drive. Motivation that fades quickly.

Curious

- "What is the source of your good intentions?" Listen for external motivations, people pleasing and other-oriented sources of motivation.
- "Are intentions creating the intended outcomes?" Listen for loose linkages in their mind between their behavior and results.
- "How are you turning intention into action?" Look for internal drive toward clear process and methodical, sustained efforts across time.
- "Do you have time to do this work? If not, where is the time going?" Watch for a lot of time being spent in coordination with the team, consensus building, getting feedback. These behaviors are likely rooted in disempowering fear, self-doubt or lack of skill and character.

- "Are you anxious about what to do or your ability to do it?"
- "What is the level and source of your internal motivations?" Much more on motivations in chapters seven and eight.

Clear

- Self leadership means connecting intention and action for yourself. Now and again, now. Forever.
- "How do you decide which decisions require team coordination and which you can make on your own?" A lot of consensus building and team coordination efforts might cover for a lack of confidence, strength or self leadership.
- "Do you have a skills development road map you are using?" Support them in methodically building ability and confidence each day using a Self Development Road Map (template available on the humane leadership website).

Constructive

- "What skills will you develop in what order? By when? When shall we check in on your progress?"
- "Do you see any opportunities to strengthen your practices of the humane leadership values of fair strength, wise balance and generative care?" Watch for a lack of agency, discipline or hope. Ask gently if they would like to work on those deeper challenges using work as

a safe laboratory. Use the Humane Leadership Values Wisdom Jig to begin this process.

- Use the Hindrances Wisdom Jig to identify goals, related risks and how they might be mitigated.
- Use the Motivations Wisdom Jig to discover more internal, hope-based sources.

Edge 12: Surrendered Self Leadership

Some of us choose not to ride the bicycle of our own lives, we take our hands off the handle bars and feet off the pedals and complain about the ride. We surrender ourselves to the direction and pace of others. The roots of learned helplessness can run very deep, but we can support behavioral choices that reengage and re-empower our teammates if they are willing to try.

Signs of Surrendered Self Leadership:

- Disengaged and blaming others– "You tell me what to do, my brain hurts." TLDR and other self-infantilizing statements.
- "They…"– feeling victimized
- Reluctance to step into adult thought and action– "I will see where life takes me, it will wash over me and float me downstream" or "How would I know?"
- Cynicism– exploiting the company by being disengaged, barely meeting lowest expectations to maintain employment, phoning it in.

- Overload and indecision– freezing up seeing so many options, avoiding narrowing choices, letting fate decide by procrastinating until choices are made by others.
- Waiting passively– for a sign, authority, time to unfold, permission.

Curious– ask:

- "What do you want?"
- "What seems worth doing?"
- "What are you waiting for?"
- "What can you do without permission?"
- "Who can you connect with to learn more?"
- "What tiny first step might lead you to more clarity?"
- "What are you afraid of?"– explore with Root Cause Analysis Wisdom Jig.

Clear

- "Do you feel like you have agency in your life? We can experiment with that if you'd like. It is your life..."
- Focus on building momentum and choosing direction– get their feet on the pedals and their hands on the handlebars of their own life. Momentum is the key to moving forward and maintaining your balance. Start pedaling. Direction can be adjusted once you are in motion, balanced, and learning as you move.
- Every moment is an opportunity to choose to try again, to experiment anew. Each moment is a tipping point,

leading up towards rewarding experiences and edification or leading down to disappointment, disempowerment and depression.

- Dopamine loops are for you to design for your own long term benefit.

Constructive

- Directions– pick one to start. Build some momentum, then reevaluate after you have covered some new territory.
- Momentum is more important than knowing exactly where you are going.
- Experiments– boldness, counter-phobic, dopamine
- Find others who are active self leaders and hang out with them. You are the average of the five people you spend most time with. Choose wisely and courageously.

Edge 13: Personal Issues

Humane leadership seeks to address the entire human being. And of course, we cannot separate performance on the job from our people's human challenges and experiences. Humane leaders must carefully balance the desire to hold the whole human being without being hobbled by persistent personal issues.

Signs of personal issues:

- Missed time.
- Emotional neediness– requiring a lot of time to process.
- Insecurity or distorted sense of themselves and their role in the world.
- Anger or despairing reactions to common work situations.
- Needy family, friends, or pets that interfere via phone, text, or time off.

Curious– ask:

- "Are you okay?"
- "Will this resolve soon? What will change?"
- "Can we (the team, the organization) help in some way?"
- "How do you feel about this situation?"– personally or its impact on their work.
- "Do you understand how this affects the team?"

Clear

- "This is actually important to resolve before it affects your performance any further."

- "The team needs you to fill this role and bring your most positive energy to our work and culture."
- "We can be supportive in the short term, but soon the team will need to have you back. How can I support you in returning to full capacity?"
- "Let's set a time to check in on your progress to resolve this situation." Set that time halfway to the date that they say the situation will be resolved so that you can get a sense of progress and drive changes required to resolve the matter as agreed. Don't allow so much time that the person has space to fail because of your neglect.
- Avoid taking any responsibility for resolving the issue for the person, only offer to support their efforts and join the steps they are initiating themselves. This will ensure you have an empowered team member returning to full capacity rather than a weak player whose return to continued underperformance you enabled.

Constructive

- Offer your support and coaching on resolving the situation.
- Offer all the benefits the company or the community offers that might help the person.
- "Let's work together to keep this from becoming a corrective action situation. I think the two of us can handle this."
- Offer to use the hindrances or performance jigs to help them clarify their next steps.

First, don't dig into personal failings unless you have clear consent to do so, but do talk about anything that impacts their work performance. For instance, if someone is regularly arriving late and bleary-eyed on Monday mornings, you can note that behavior and how it impacts their team and work without stepping into your suspicions about their self-destructive habits.

It is important to support, but not coddle. We must ask people, once the crisis moment is past, to live out of our shared values of fair strength and wise balance. Leaders are the ones who have been chosen to step into, not avoid, these sensitive, crucial conversations.

In modern American culture, some people who are caring and compassionate and sensitive feel the need to process those feelings with others. This can be a lovely, humane experience, but it may also conflict with the needs of the team.

Our focus on compassion does not mean that we must all share in each other's suffering. People who are suffering should, to the extent possible, be compassionate to their team members. There's an old Prussian virtue, "Learn to suffer without complaining." This is an antidote to the cliche that misery loves company. The line between compassion and sharing suffering in a way that burdens and disempowers others is a fine one that requires mindful introspection and wisdom to navigate.

Some misery needs company and compassion, but you may find a team member habitually recruiting others to share in their turmoil or sadness in ways that are inappropriate. Leaders must help those who are not seeing how their sharing of suffering is unfair to others. It is the leader's job to gently but clearly ask the person to have compassion for the needs of the team or clients. In fact, serving others in the midst of our own suffering can be therapeutic because, like all work, it helps us transcend ourselves if only for an hour or two.

Our values of fair strength and wise balance call us, even in our suffering, to contribute to our team's goals. **And,** we are humans, so we know that we will all have days with extra needs. Your regular performance review one-on-one meetings and the humane leadership values set the stage for this otherwise awkward conversation.

If the person is really oblivious, willing to live in denial, and unable to speak about what's really difficult and true for them, ask yourself:

- Is your team served by working with this person?
- Can you effectively lead that kind of a person?
- Might this person be served by finding a better place to work through their issues?

If the person needs to find another team to work on while they sort through their personal challenges, the last sections of this chapter might help you with that process. You could also enlist your human resources department's help to free the person to pursue other opportunities.

Edge 14: Freedom Fighter

Many adults simply crave freedom as an end in itself.

On our career path, we may see the way before us all too clearly.

As we see the well-defined track, something within us balks or surges. We know we must be free.

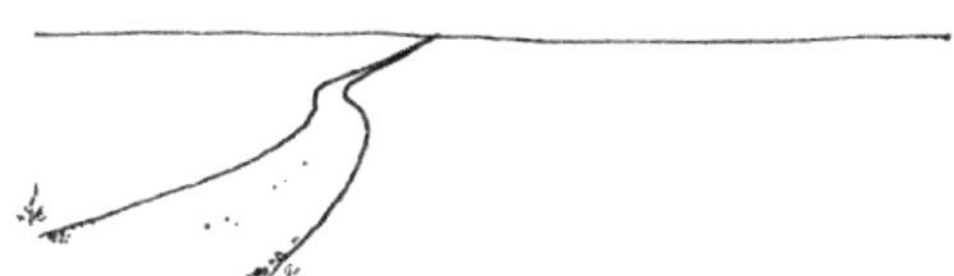

Sometimes these feelings are conscious, but often they are not. Leaders who have yearned for freedom themselves can spot the early signs in members of their team: bucking the system, stuck in the doldrums, or frustrated with the daily realities of teamwork.

This may be a natural result of being an intelligent, capable human being. In fact, E M. Forster wrote a wonderful story called "The Other Side of the Hedge" about this experience.

> At first I thought it was going to be like my brother, whom I had had to leave by the roadside a year or two around the corner. He had wasted his breath on singing, and his strength on helping others. But I had traveled more wisely, and now it was only the monotony of the highway that oppressed me– dust under foot and brown crackling hedges on either side, ever since I could remember.

Wise leaders can sometimes spot Freedom Fighters even before they are aware of their own needs for self-actualization and creative fulfillment.

Signs that you may have a Freedom Fighter:

- Prioritizing autonomy and creative license.
- Ignoring social norms and lacking temperance.
- Rebelling against systems, processes and rules.
- Shying from accountability.
- Ignoring the fun in having rules and discipline; the net and lines on the court help make tennis fun.

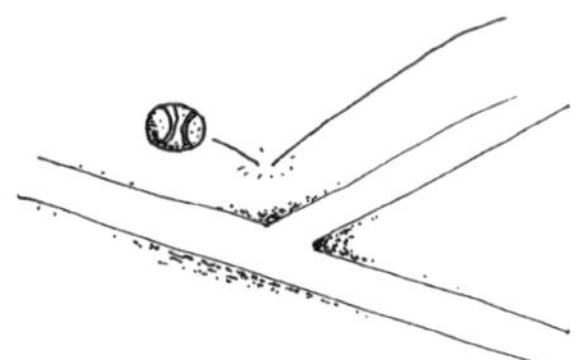

- Unwilling to live the values of fair strength and wise balance.

Curious– you can ask:

- "What do you love about this work?"
- "What do you love even more than this work?"
- "What's keeping you from pursuing your passions full time?"
- "What do you need that you're not getting here?"
- "What would need to change for you to find fulfillment here?"
- "How can we give you more autonomy to experiment?
- "What would you like to experiment with to improve performance?"
- "How can I help you get closer to your goal?"

- "Is this team the right place for you? How shall we think about returning you to freedom of choice around your work?"

Clear– you can say:

- "This role and our team require certain outputs and that service level agreements be kept. For instance, we need x quality of response within y time after a request."
- "Do you need more freedom to work effectively?"
- "I want to support you because I appreciate you as a human being, but I must ensure that the team gets what it needs each day."
- "You are a free adult. You may choose any path you want in life, but on this team, only a few options are available. I am happy to explore those with you as long as we can meet the needs of the team."

Constructive

- "Let's design an experiment to see how your creative freedom can support the team's goals"
- Agree on a mechanism and a cadence for assessing these experiments with changes to systems and processes. The cadence should include at least a monthly team check in on the experiment's progress.
- Create a continuous chain of creative projects to harness the revolutionary energy to improve the team's work.

- "If we can't align our needs and goals, how can we support your next steps toward freedom beyond this role?"

The leader must hold firm to the truth that the flipside of the coin of liberty is responsibility.

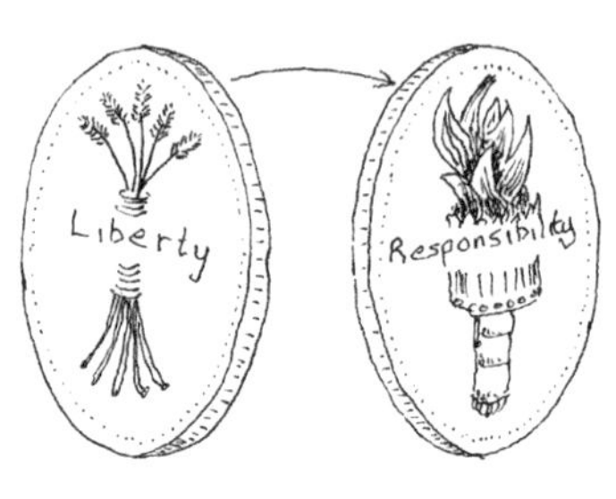

As leaders, we can start functional adult workers with a fair amount of liberty or looseness. If they use their liberty responsibly, they get to keep their liberty. If they do not meet performance expectations, then we as leaders must tighten up accountability. This is the essential lesson of the biblical parable of the talents, which is almost like a mantra:

> The person who can be trusted with little,
> will be trusted with much.

As leaders, we are trusted with the engagement of our team's desire for creative contribution and emergence. We must offer people a living balance of the freedom they desire and the structure they need to meet their own and the team's needs.

Leaders good with balancing liberty and responsibility for their teams know, as Howard Thurman wrote, "what the world needs is people who have come alive."

Having a team of people who are fully alive will create a vital working experience for us as leaders as well. This is the regenerative promise of humane leadership.

Of course, Freedom Fighters are not always focused on doing what's most efficient or conducive to team cohesion. Some of us just aren't suited to structure. I have a friend, fresh out of art school, who worked at a large, midwestern firm with a formal dress code. When told that the code required that men wear ties to work, he headed to Goodwill after work and arrived the next morning with two distinctly unattractive ties around his neck. He soon left the firm and has maintained his personal and artistic freedom ever since.

At least the rebel is being honest about their needs and intentions. Our next challenge is harder to spot because it is not so honest.

Edge 15: Passive Aggressive

Sometimes the first person to enthusiastically agree to a new idea is the person we end up having the most trouble with. This person often starts off more agreeable than honest. Later, they can't continue the lie and they begin to quietly undermine or attack your team's efforts.

Passive aggressive people avoid being courageous, clear and honest about their anger. To avoid confrontation, they work via back channels to meet their own needs.

Signs of Passive Aggressive behavior:

- Eager to agree, even without the details or full understanding of the request. The details will be disregarded soon enough, so why worry about them now?
- May start with the best of intentions, but you will soon sense an edge to their compliance.
- Silent, sullen, resigned or bitter. "It's fine. I have nothing to add."
- Delayed redelegation– handing work back to the person who requested it after some time has passed with no real progress made.
- Pessimism– it's all a *$@! Storm, a cluster, dumpster fire, FUBAR or SNAFU
- Positioning themselves as the unsung hero or the one who knew it wouldn't work all along.
- Declaring themselves the victim of deception or being misunderstood and unappreciated.

Curious

- Ask for their suggestions on the toughest details in your plan. This calls them to be thoughtful, clear, and on the record about important details before they can disengage from them.
- Ask for their opinion if they are being silent, sullen, resigned or bitter. Ask in a private meeting, "What's concerning you about this? Do you feel that your opinion doesn't count? Have you felt deceived in some

way? What can I do to show you that I value your thinking?"

- If they redelegate, ask, "What changed between the time I gave you this task and when you brought it back to me? How can you avoid doing this in the future?"
- If they persist in avoidance and secret aggressions, call a private meeting and ask, "Are you feeling justified in making things uncomfortable for the team? Why? Should we talk about the root cause of those reasons and the beliefs behind them?" Pull in an HR representative if you think this might go off track.

Clear

- "We need everyone pulling in the same direction. I need you to figure out how you can get on board. I need a written plan for improved performance from you by *x* date."
- "Let's get clear about which of your needs are not being met. Frustration is an indicator of some unmet need or a violated value. This matters to me, so let's work directly on that so you can be engaged and clear." Search "Nonviolent communication needs list" online for a list of needs that might be unmet. You as leader cannot allow a passive aggressive person to hide out and quietly undermine your team's performance.
- "Because the team needs to move quickly and clearly, I need for you to practice clarifying and clearly communicating your needs to me and your teammates as we are in the decision making and planning processes.

What can you agree with me about the clarity and timeliness of your communication?"

- If they have felt deceived, dig into that experience. Deception implies intent, so ask, "Who do you think deceived you? Why do you think they would want to do that? Why does that seem true? What if it wasn't true? How can we learn if the person really intended to do that?"

Constructive

- "It's important to me and to the team that we understand your contributions, so please keep a list of the contributions you are making that we can discuss in our one-on-one meetings."
- Take responsibility for anything you did as a leader to create their sense of disempowerment. Do what you can to make things better, but do not accept responsibility for any pattern of self-disempowerment and cynicism they are bringing to the table.
- "When I delegate something to you, I need you to dig in right away to clarify everything you'll need to get it done as planned. I need your help so we can learn how to do these handoffs really well."
- "I'm not interested in easy agreement or avoiding conflict; I'm interested in finding the truth about creating the most value possible each day. So if you find yourself not agreeing, I need you to step in. Don't nod your head to avoid conflict. You don't need to create a scene, just say to me, 'Let's talk about that before we

take any next steps'. Then, we will dig in and all learn something. If we need to schedule a follow up time because it's a bigger issue, we'll do that."

- Ask them to lead the testing and refinement of the work they are cynical or pessimistic about. Ideally, they should lead the team responsible to stress test and derisk the project or process.

This might seem like handing control of your agenda to the passive aggressive person, but it is not. Giving them responsibility for risks calls their bluff, which works because passive aggressive people are often heroes in their own minds, but cowards socially. In response to your clarity, they will likely either get on board, make their questions and suggestions snappy or move along to another team because your clarity and openness scares them away. All are desirable outcomes for you and your team.

If the passive aggressive person requires a lot of time to handle irrelevant concerns, that becomes a different conversation about their ability and relevance. At least the passive aggressive behavior has evaporated at that point.

Remember, the goal is not to keep everyone on your team; the goal is to keep the best people on your team performing well.

Story: A Performance Challenge in Practice

To give you a sense of what P(MOCA) looks like in practice, here is a story from our recent client work with the leader of a firm that was performing well below its potential. The company had a stable and skilled team, but their work was not fully fruitful for clients or profitable for the firm.

The leader was frustrated because the team's profitability was being diverted from e-commerce development into unbilled client and administrative work. The leader had two other businesses at the same time so he needed the team to create client value more autonomously rather than demand daily management.

I started by asking questions about the ratio of client hours and administrative work to the retainers being billed to the customers. The senior developer introduced a number of ambiguities to the situation and grudgingly made a couple of symbolic attempts to tinker with the allocation of time. The leader's frustration was rising while the team seemed agreeable but was actually hiding the truth and digging in their heels. Tensions rose as time drifted by.

Rather than step into the conflict, I shifted the conversation by introducing the Performance Wisdom Jig.

I started by walking through the model in a theoretical way. Then I asked them to use the tool to evaluate themselves privately.

Behaving a bit passive aggressively, the senior developer and team "forgot" to do the self evaluation for a couple of weeks. We asked politely and consistently each week, and eventually, after realizing that we would not accept avoidance, the team completed their self evaluations.

The leader and I then met privately with each team member so that the leader could see how I held the staff members and the performance evaluation as a collaborative, experimental search for truth.

It felt like we turned a corner when the senior developer, working with us through his self evaluation asked if he could use the tool to improve his guitar practice as well. Of course, the Performance Wisdom Jig works on any human performance. His face brightened and we set to work with renewed vigor to identify small adjustments that would improve performance.

These were not permanent changes to start, but were set up as experiments worth trying for a week or two. The senior developer was having difficulty hearing clients on the telephone, so we chose to experiment with a headset that covered both ears and had a volume control. We understood that this was likely a diversion from the core issues involved, but, for a small investment, we were able to call his bluff.

At the same time, we asked if the senior developer could schedule all his client work time blocks starting on Monday morning and front load the week so that time was left to address emergencies and emergent opportunities as the week unfolded. We started this second experiment and continued to look for additional performance improvements to experiment with. Experiments are not permanent, they are simply creative ways of collaboratively seeking the truth about better performance.

As we collaborated with team members to convert more experiments into process improvements, the level of reluctance fell and everyone could see that the leader's interests were clear and honest. It also helped that the team saw their own ideas making a real difference. Soon, the team warmed to the idea that this was not a zero-sum game, it was a collaborative and creative reengineering process that could make the experience and profitability of work improve in tandem. A velvet revolution had begun.

Over several weeks the team changed how they scheduled their work. They freed up hours to develop their skills and to implement new tools and processes. The changes boosted efficiency and allowed them to focus on more valuable, energizing creative tasks.

In the end the staff asked to learn a Socratic consulting methodology we'd used to help them support clients in identifying and prioritizing future projects. Suddenly the developers had become valuable consultants to both clients and the firm out of their choice and desire to learn. Productivity, profitability, staff engagement, and customer satisfaction all rose dramatically. The firm was healthy and fruitful at last without any weeping or gnashing of teeth.

Edge 16: Overly Aggressive

What if the person leaves passive stealth behind and shows up as simply aggressive?

Aggressive people often have passing lane energies; "I'm going to hit the gas, swerve over, shift gears and leave you suckers in the dust!" They may require others to adjust their behavior and values or they may blatantly pursue a promotion ahead of everyone around them.

If the aggressive person is super capable and relevant to the organization, this energy shift can be great. The team may benefit by learning new approaches to their work and moving at a faster tempo. But we must be careful to avoid long-term damage to the team's cohesion and productivity in exchange for short term adjustments to the aggressive person's style.

The organization may best be served by letting the aggressive person pass you all. If the person is honorable, then you as their supportive former leader may have an ally who's moving quickly through the organization. Unfortunately, that is often not the case.

There's nothing more damaging to an organization than a half-educated, action-oriented leader.

One dark side of aggressive people is that they start running in mistaken directions and just do, do, do. While their action orientation is very satisfying to them personally and seems like progress for the team at first, it could do great damage over time.

Why So Aggressive?

The question is, what is the source of all of this energy? Are they actually trying to serve the organization or are they proving something to themselves?

> We almost always have something to prove when we act heroically. We prove to ourselves and others that we are not what we and others thought we were. Our real self is petty, greedy, cowardly, dishonest and stewing

> in malice. And now in defying death and spitting in its eye we grasp at the chance of a grand refutation.
>
> — Eric Hoffer, American philosopher

Rather than serving the team, the grand refutation is that opportunity to fill the void of insecurity with a great accomplishment. This source of motivation is usually tremendously destructive to a team's morale and alignment.

Humane leaders help align people's personal motivations with the needs of the organization. This alignment can energize all the work of a team, pull it forward, and raise the level of play for everybody.

It's like an orchestra; having a really great player can draw the entire orchestra forward. But, if the first trumpet is a powerful player and suddenly improvises a solo in the middle of the piece, well, that could be quite disruptive. The leader must orchestrate the players to serve the piece that the team has agreed to play.

Signs of an aggressive person are:

- Obviously seeking to earn influence with people in, around, and above the team.
- Clamoring for visibility before they earn influence by being relevant and unique.
- Armed with a clearly defined persona and even props. They may come in and actually seem to be wearing a costume of some kind, wearing power suits, or being a self described "type A." I've heard a senior female

business leader describe herself as a "chihuahua with a bone." She even brought her own talisman of authority to every meeting, a plastic sandwich bag of memory sticks she claimed were filled with the latest academic HR research compiled by a team of anonymous graduate students she retained. "Expertise, check!"

- Sources of frustration and upset in the good, diligent core of the firm. The core people who have been with the organization a long time can either be stabilizing ballast for the ship or barnacles on the hull that slow the ship down. The aggressive person will see the core as barnacles, but the leader's job is to discern when the core people are actually ballast. As ballast, they keep the ship steady in the storms of reality. The aggressive person will see them as frustrating, freeloading obstructions. Great leaders hold this healthy tension and orchestrate the balance between the wisdom of the ages and the exciting promise of the new.

Curious

- "What is your goal here? How do you see that aligned with the team's goals?"
- "How can I support you?"
- "Is the team supporting you?" In their answer, does the person have a realistic, humane assessment of the team's role?
- "At what cost to yourself (others, the team) are you pursuing your goal?"

- "If you were in charge, what would we be doing? Are you seeing problems with our current plan? If so, what are they and how would you solve them?" Pay attention to this assessment to see if it is fully formed, balanced and supportable. Is this person half educated?
- "What are you noticing about the culture of the team and organization?" Look closely at the balance and subtle perceptiveness of this assessment. Are they just being dismissive, seeing people as pawns or cogs in a machine to serve their own needs?
- "What are your favorite, most influential sources of wisdom?" A tip off would be "myself" or some dogma-based authority. Look for the nuance and humility built into the answer here.
- "How do you balance internal and external motivations?" Listen for the deeper sources of their motivation and the nuance of their self awareness here.

Clear

- "On this team, we seek first to understand and then to be understood."
- "We have a plan. Your best path to earning influence is to help us deliver on the plan. You could help us refine, but not replace the plan this year."
- "I have learned that sometimes the most powerful person is the quietest. To know where that is true, we must watch and listen carefully."
- "Skilled adults work by choice for their own, internal motivations. How we uncover people's motivations is

very important to the culture of this team. I think you might enjoy looking more closely at your own sources of motivation."

- "This team is an orchestra and even the lead trumpet doesn't choose when to blast out a solo. That's destructive to the art we've all agreed to make here."
- "I am responsible for the success of the entire team. So please align yourself with that and we will do great things together."

Constructive

- Create a plan for the person's contributions. Give them aligned opportunities to shine within your plans.
- Discuss Plato's Allegory of the Charioteer as a model for humility and empathy that acknowledges the challenges of coordinating our highest aspirations and the harder realities of our humanity.
- "If you would like extra opportunities, let me know and I will work to open doors to new projects, skills and opportunities for you that serve the organization's needs **and** your personal needs."
- "If you cannot align with the team's goals, let me know right away and I will try to find a great new opportunity for you; a role where you will be more free to make your unique impact."
- Discuss the humane leadership values of fair strength, wise balance and generative care. "The artful coordination of all of these lived character qualities is what

makes a great leader and will maximize your positive impact on this team over time."

- Teach the person to earn influence using the Earning Influence Wisdom Jig. Help them develop relevant skills that they can apply to making unique contributions to the large goal that everyone is working towards. That is what will maximize their influence over time and minimize their conflict with the organization.

Recently, I was working with a large software firm in Silicon Valley, when a young, freshly-minted MBA came into a department whose leader felt threatened by her energy and clarity. With no warning, he gave her a negative review that made her ineligible for stock options. Obviously, she felt upset and was even considering legal action. Another leader in the firm, my point of contact, was mentoring this woman. She heard her concerns, reported this abusive treatment of a valuable employee, and took her onto her own team.

I advised the new leader as the energetic young woman joined her team. We talked about how a leader can help a powerful person earn influence while creating a strong ally in the organization. The mentor identified opportunities for the young woman to apply her unique skills to an important question relevant to senior leadership. Then, the mentor scheduled the young woman to present her ideas to the senior leadership team.

By supporting her earned influence, the mentor transformed a person on the verge of filing a lawsuit into an important contributor to the firm.

Only the leader can hold these edges of the team, from the aggressive person who tries to override the team to the star player who refuses to play by the team's rules. How we maintain and shape these edges defines the performance of our team and our own character as leaders.

The Leader Defines the Edges

Recently, the New York Times reported on a leadership crisis at the New York City Ballet.

"The country's premier ballet company, which has defined grace, speed and precision since the days of its co-founder George Balanchine, is now also a stage for the era's #MeToo convulsions" (NY Times). The ballet looked to hire a new "humane leader."

Principal dancer Ashley Bouder wrote on Instagram, "May we find a moral and fair individual to lead us out of this darkness and into future respect, integrity and success."

This new leader would need to create an environment that incorporates: "a culture of equal respect for all...common decency...a moral compass...a more nurturing environment...a more open culture...an anonymous complaint system...annual performance evaluations...more counseling for mental health, substance abuse, performance anxiety and nutrition" and "safe working environments."

How exactly does a leader create such a humane environment?

At the New York City Ballet, and in any organization, the leader sets and hosts what Dutch historian and cultural theorist Johan Huizinga likens to a "game" each day. The leader of the game sets the environment, physically, socially, and culturally.

Within this environment, the leader invites or removes the players/actors. In a ballet this would be dancers and choreographers, but also bookkeepers, board members, and maintenance people. Relationships between all the participants must also be established and held by the leader. This process requires that the leader decide: Is the company just the dancers? Does it include the staff too? Does the game include the Board of Directors? Key donors? The audience? Which segments of the wider community? Where and how clearly these lines are drawn profoundly affect the experience of everyone involved.

Humane leaders work with all the actors involved to develop a clear, shared set of rules. Where there is ambiguity, the leader hosts conversations to bring clarity and alignment.

The #MeToo movement has exposed leaders and organizations to fresh judgment under a more enlightened set of rules. Not only are the rules changing, but some team members are now demanding more control over which actors get to continue playing.

Sometimes humane leaders must clarify rules and remove anyone not willing or able to play by the shared rules, even if the errant person is a star or a key donor. This is a service to everyone in the organization.

If the leader tries to play nice with errant people and not hold them to account, they are often sowing the seeds for abuse, injustice and potential destruction of the entire organization.

Lack of fair strength in the leader can create an abusive and exploitative, an inhumane, workplace.

Typically, teams cannot hold the rules by themselves. In the absence of a strong leader who holds the entire game in the best interests of the group, entropy of consciousness will allow lowest denominator standards and short-term self interests to undermine the group's cohesion and effectiveness.

While holding the team and the rules, the humane leader will then host conversations about prioritizing and implementing the clear, nurturing, supportive ideas the team has voiced.

May you hold your team's edges with fair strength, generative care and wise balance.

When Performance Doesn't Improve

Sometimes, leaders must remove entire trees to protect the fruitfulness of their orchards because pruning and shaping around the edges of a tree is not enough.

A leader's job is to match people and opportunities, not to hold opportunities open for people who can't or won't seize them for the benefit of all. Opportunities are valuable and scarce, so leaders must distribute them to optimize for the growth of the people on the team and for the performance the organization requires. Humane leaders balance the needs of the organization and the team with the needs of individuals who might be struggling to perform well in their current roles.

Sometimes good intentions are not enough. You may have a person who has the greatest intentions and is quite lovable, but has difficulty delivering the appropriate actions at the appropriate time. They may talk about and hope for self control, but when things get tough, they get snarky or worse. We can talk, they can apologize and make promises, but they may not be able to keep the promises they make.

The team may not be the best place for the person to sort out the intellectual, habitual, or emotional challenges undermining their effectiveness and civil behavior. At the end of the day, the team requires performance and behavior aligned with its aspirations. A leader must protect the needs of the team while being as compassionate as possible with each person. In the end, it might be most compassionate to help the person find a more natural team and role for themselves.

When someone is not quite fitting with the role and team, you'll start noticing simple symptoms of underperformance.

- Good intentions but failure to thrive.
- Avoidance or passive aggressive behavior.
- Tasks missed or handed back partially completed.

Unfortunately, it's highly unlikely that a person who is living out the Peter Principle (promoted to their level of incompetence) will proactively resolve the situation themselves. Underperformers will often put a friendly face on their subpar results, disengagement, and internal misery, but they are unlikely to quit. Most underperforming employees don't have the clarity about themselves and their options in the world to quit jobs they are not suited for. Helping them move on is the leader's job.

People with strength, vision, and initiative quit unsuitable jobs, the rest will linger as long as leaders let them.

The oft-cited Gallup poll shows that 70% of all employees in North America are disengaged at work. Those 70% are lingering in your organization busily underperforming.

Luckily, we can use the Performance Wisdom Jig to address this underperformance epidemic. Working through the variables with underperformers, we'll learn whether performance challenges can be overcome.

Once you have clarified the expectations, time, and authority issues and performance still doesn't improve, it's best to focus on ability. It's usually quite clear if a person has some specific skills or habits to develop. If the person simply falls short of the innate talent required to perform well, adding motivation only delays the inevitable role change the leader must initiate.

After looking at all that, if the employee is honest, they may confess a lack of motivation (or even helplessness) to change their performance. They may say "That's just the way I am, I doubt I'll ever change."

That may be acceptable to them, but it's not okay for the team, its performance, and its culture. It is frustrating to be slowed down by a struggling team mate and it is demoralizing for everyone to see a role and its related opportunities wasted on someone who doesn't or can't honor them.

If motivation is the issue, the leader could say, "I could create some fearsome consequences if you don't meet the standards, but that's not the way I want to work with you. I'm committed to working as a humane leader. What would make you want to perform well?" Hopefully the person can get to a place of pride and contribution, engagement with their fellow workers, wanting to make a difference in the world, or learning something new. This step is about finding an internal, hope-based motivation rather than an external, fear-based consequence. Much more on this in the next chapter.

If the person cannot imagine an internal, hope-based motivation for themselves (the leaders should not step in to save a person struggling to find their own motivations), then the leader should confess to the person, "We probably need to start discussing where else you might be most fruitful on this team or in this organization."

Planning Transitions

Once it is clear a person needs to leave the team, it is important to prioritize the needs of the firm and team in transition planning. To serve the firm and the person moving on requires careful planning and a balancing of needs with ethical and policy decisions. Letting a person go is a change that must be carefully planned and managed unless there's a safety issue.

Never release someone when you feel like it, release them when it makes sense for the firm. Quietly collect the information you will need to minimize impacts on the team and any affected clients. Plan your communications with the person losing their job in a humane way by focusing on the person and their needs in the transition while never stepping away from the inevitability of the transition itself.

The Conversation: Releasing Humanely

In these difficult moments of transition, the kindest thing to do is to take the band aid off quickly and say your one sentence. "We're letting you go today." Pause to let the message land.

The key is to deliver the news quickly and clearly, then turn to the work of helping the person understand that you value them as a human being and how the next steps in your organization's process work. After that news has been delivered the person should be assured that they have good qualities that need to find an appropriate place to develop. Once the emotions of the moment are met, felt and addressed with as authentic as possible affirmation, you can work through your HR procedures for the transition.

If the person wants more clarity on reasons why, be careful to comply with your HR policies, but you will have a long relationship with the person and the issues given your weeks working on performance improvement with them, so you might say,

> "It's not anything against you. We love you. We love 'this' about you and 'that' about you, but as we've discussed, this team is not the appropriate place for you to work."
>
> "I've tried to work this situation out with you. We've had a number of meetings and conversations. But now, improvement is not moving quickly enough for the needs of the organization." N.B. Not the needs of the team– make it the organization. Citing the organization reduces the tendency to blame individuals.

> "The hardest part of my job is that I am the one who gets to have these difficult conversations with people. Unfortunately, you and I are having this conversation today."
>
> "We want our workplace to be a place of healing and growth for as many people as possible. We've given you a chance to do that here, and now it's time for you to do that elsewhere."

The key is to make your affirmative statements, but never engage in conversations about why and what if. This is a hard conversation to have, but it can be done in a very clear and affirming way, always holding open the possibility for the person to improve, **elsewhere.**

We can offer hope and support by saying, "When you are able to resolve this, we'll consider having you back because your ability to do x, y and z is tremendous." You just focus on all the positives and point out that the negative, unfortunately, despite their best intentions, it is still too much for the firm to handle.

Warm Accountability: The Greatest Challenge

One of the great challenges of humane leadership is how to hold people warmly while they are bumping into their personal edges and constraints to performance. Humane leaders assume that warmth will often be the best path toward better results. But, at the same time, humane leaders are not shy about stepping clearly and directly into the challenges of subpar performance.

Further Reading

- Forster, *The Other Side of the Hedge*, 1911
- Hoffer, *The True Believer*, 1951
- NY Times, "Who Should Run City Ballet? A Job Posting, Explained," August 14, 2018
- Plato, "Allegory of the Charioteer" in the dialog *Phaedrus* (sections 246a–254e)
- Rosenberg, Search "Nonviolent communication needs list"
- Rosenberg, *Non-Violent Communication*, 2003

Sources of Motivation

All performance follows a breaking of inertia to **do** something.

To improve performance, we need to help people discover their own sustainable desire to freely choose action and improvement. Leaders can clarify expectations and develop people's skills, but in the end we are faced with the challenge of the wavering, fragile sources of motivation in the humans we lead.

Of course, many people resort to the use of fear-based motivations like, "Do it, or else." That's where I grew up.

Perhaps the most egregious example of this approach was in the late 1980s, when an Eastern Airlines management representative leading labor negotiations was quoted saying about staff motivation, "We use the carrot and stick routine. We take the carrot and shove it. Then we use the stick to tamp it in." Is it any wonder that these negotiations ended in Eastern Airlines' bankruptcy and dissolution?

Unfortunately, fear-based motivations are inhumane to the worker, exhausting and demoralizing to the leader, and culturally unsustainable over time. Can we find sources of motivation that are hope-based, edifying and humane to all involved?

Experiment: Internal, Hope-Based Motivations

Before trying to motivate others, humane leaders will first experiment to identify their own internal, hope-based sources of motivation. Using the resulting compassion, clarity, and depth of motivation gained, the leader can then help others explore and strengthen their own sources of motivation.

Luckily, we motivate and lead ourselves throughout each day so we have a lot of opportunities to experiment. I call this our self leadership laboratory; discreet, immediate, and fully equipped to teach us about leading humans.

You led yourself to get out of bed this morning. Was it from an internal, natural motivation or an external fear-based forcing function like being late or missing a deadline? Ideally, we'd get up with a hope-based, internal motivation based on what difference we'd love to make in the world.

To explore your own sources of motivation, try this experiment: Don't get out of bed tomorrow until you arise naturally out of an internal, hope-based motivation. If you need to use the bathroom, please do that and then immediately return to bed to begin your experiment.

Notice what comes up in your mind and body as you lie awake in bed.

- Do you feel ashamed?
- Are you afraid of someone else shaming you?
- Do you feel weak or useless?
- Are you doubting yourself as a competent person?
- Do you feel the pressure of a hundred undone tasks?
- Whose voices are you hearing speaking these thoughts?
- Is your body just itching to get going?

Let this all float downstream. Notice it all, but do not accept them as motivations yet. Stay in bed as you search for and allow an internal hope-based motivation to arise. Ask yourself:

- Who do I aspire to be this day?
- What could I happily work on today?
- How would I feel if I did those things all day?
- Which task on my list today moves me towards an inspiring goal?

In my experience, I will be thinking about these questions and suddenly I will find that I have already jumped out of bed and started my morning routine. I've just discovered an internal, hope-based source of motivation.

Notice a few more things before you start your day:

- How long did it take for you to spontaneously arise?
- What were you thinking and feeling just before you popped out of bed?
- What of note might you experiment with tomorrow?
- Are you exhausted and falling back to sleep? What can you learn from that?
- Are you still in bed? How long has it been?
- Are you feeling hopelessness, shame, or fear?

If you didn't learn anything in twenty minutes today except that there's no good reason to get up and you didn't get in trouble with anyone, that's important data and a very interesting start. Get up and start your day. Try the experiment each morning until you find something internal and hope-based that consistently gets you going.

Experimentation is just seeking what's true, why it might be true, and what it might mean for our lives.

You can continue your experiment throughout the day. Keep noticing your sources of motivation as they rise and fall. I sometimes just ask myself the question, "Why?" at various times during the day to collect more motivations data as I work.

Brazilian businessman Ricardo Semler takes this experiment to great lengths. He keeps his Mondays and Thursdays as "Terminal Days." He schedules nothing and is present to what he would want to do on those days if he had just received a terminal medical diagnosis. This practice empowers his own internal, hope-based motivations in 40% of his working week! That is a fascinating and empowering experiment in humane self leadership. I wonder how much of his obvious privilege he earned by being so committed to self and team leadership experiments.

By doing your own smaller experiment, you may notice that you have a tendency to respond well to external fear-based motivations or give less credence to internal hope-based motivations. You may notice the feeling that an external fear-based motivation leaves in your body. You may feel somewhat manipulated by that external force. Do you feel like a self-actualizing creative human being when you are responding to external fear?

Here's a wisdom jig designed to help you examine and experiment with your sources of motivation.

Sources of Motivation Wisdom Jig

Hope

Fear

External

Internal

Instructions for this Wisdom Jig:

1. Download a pdf of this jig from our website or use a piece of paper.
2. Notice what sources of motivations arise in the course of your experiments or just think about your motivational habits and list what you find. Add each to the appropriate box in the jig. You may want to check in on your levels and sources of motivation a number of times per day over a few days to collect a more complete set of data points.
3. Once you have a fairly complete list, circle those that are most powerful or habitual for you.
4. Look at each of the most powerful sources of motivation to see how it served, serves, or no longer serves your highest values.
5. Examine the root causes of any motivations you find mysterious or troubling. You can use the standard "5 Whys" approach or our Root Cause Analysis Wisdom Jig.
6. Design an experiment to strengthen your most powerful internal, hope-based source of motivation using the Humane Leadership Lab Notebook to structure and track your experiment.

Do you notice that giving some quiet space to your deeper sources of motivation allowed them to arise within you? My findings indicate that regular practice increases our consciousness of our motivations and reduces the time required to return to them. This all becomes clearer and more efficient with practice.

Writing this book was a multi-month experiment in shifting my daily motivations towards internal hope based authorship. In October of 2019, after nine months on a very external, exhausting, fear and greed-based client project, I decided to experiment with finding a more personal, durable, and authentic source of motivation for my next project, this book.

Here's the Sources of Motivation Wisdom Jig I used to look at the question, "Why should I write this book?"

	External	Internal
Hope	My people being proud of me	Creating valuable content so I can be free to explore my questions and to capture my paths & discoveries in words, drawing and photos.
Fear	Being irrelevant Seen as a failure Not paying my bills	Feeling like I wasted this life by not doing what I really find alive, useful and important

After a few days of digging using this wisdom jig and root cause analysis, I learned that freedom was my ultimate goal and that writing was my path to freedom. When that idea landed on the paper, I experienced a resounding "Yes." I then happily worked on the manuscript for the next six months.

Fear became only a faint echo after yelling in my ear for so many years.

Hope-based motivations activate dopamine reward loops in our brains as discussed in chapter four. Tapping into our natural, positive motivation system to create healthy habits is a powerful leadership tool.

Of course we also have fearful cortisol loops that keep us safe in crisis by activating adrenaline and other stress hormones that help our bodies defend themselves from threats. Unfortunately, most of us overuse the cortisol loop and burn ourselves and each other out. Examine your own balance and sources of dopamine and cortisol experiences using the Positive, Motivating Experience Wisdom Jig on our site.

The question is, are we passing our worst motivational habits on to our team-mates, peers, and children? We need to be careful, because we still have vestiges of old fears that reemerge in a crisis or with just a bit of disappointment and some time to worry.

We can't motivate others much differently than we motivate ourselves. As you become more aware of your own motivations, you will naturally motivate others with greater subtlety and compassion.

Please, put on your own oxygen mask before helping those around you.

Motivating One Other

We often think of motivation in terms of groups of people, almost a wholesale approach. We ask ourselves questions like:

- How can we motivate our sales team?
- Can we incent the assembly people to go faster?
- What can we do, young people aren't motivated by money the way we were?

Privileged people seeing frontline workers (referred to as "hands" from Coketown here) as a mass is not new. From 1854:

> For the first time in her life Louisa had come into one of the dwellings of the Coketown Hands; for the first time in her life she was face to face with anything like individuality in connection with them. She knew of their existence by hundreds and by thousands. She knew what results in work a given number of them would produce in a given space of time. She knew them in crowds passing to and from their nests, like ants or beetles. But she knew from her reading infinitely more of the ways of toiling insects than of these toiling men and women.
>
> Something to be worked so much and paid so much, and there ended; something to be infallibly settled by laws of supply and demand; something that blundered against those laws, and floundered into difficulty; something that was a little pinched when wheat was dear, and over-ate itself when wheat was cheap; something that increased at such a rate of percentage, and yielded such another percentage of crime, and such another percentage of pauperism; something wholesale, of which vast fortunes were

> made; something that occasionally rose like a sea, and did some harm and waste (chiefly to itself), and fell again; this she knew the Coketown Hands to be. But, she had scarcely thought more of separating them into units, than of separating the sea itself into its component drops.
>
> — Dickens, *Hard Times*

I think it is far more effective to think of individuals and their personal, internal motivations rather than groups of humans. When it comes to motivating others, some categorization and generalizations will help us think of possibilities, but, as you learned in your own experiments, sources of motivation are best sourced within an individual's private hopes and values. Internal hope cannot be pasted on from outside.

- How can we help David fulfill his desire to contribute in his new role?
- How can we align with Darlene's need to fund her daughter's college education?
- How can we help Eustice align his ecological values with his work in the factory?

This more individual focus uncovers a personal, internal hope and ties that to a desirable outcome for all involved–the person and the organization. While this work may seem time-consuming and inefficient, is it efficient to have 70% of our workers disengaged? What else are you paying front line leaders to do but support the success of their team members?

Needs of People and the Organization

Frontline leaders are paid to effectively engage, align and motivate the individuals on their team in the work and values of the organization.

Managers think in terms of span of control, humane leaders think in terms of span of connection, engagement, and generative care.

By really engaging with their people, by giving the gift of intentional attention, frontline leaders can earn the right to help them discover their own...

> ... force that through the green fuse drives the flower.
>
> — Dylan Thomas

But how can we help others learn their strongest, most personal sources of motivation? We can use the simple motivation analysis tool above as a start, but to dig deeper, you will want to help people look carefully at their own needs.

Most adults are motivated to fulfill their unmet needs. Maslow's hierarchy of needs is a good starting point to consider what those might be. Most of our workers have met their basic biological, health and safety needs. But even adults can ignore their own

need for healthy food, movement, ergonomic health and psychological safety. Other people, having met their more basic needs, are seeking a sense of belonging, esteem or creative authorship, what Maslow called self actualization.

By looking closely at my own motivations as I wrote this book, I discovered my needs for authorship and freedom, two forms of self actualization in Maslow's hierarchy.

Working from motivations based on my own needs helped me be more patient and persistent as I supported my team in exploring their own needs and motivations.

Roots of Internal Motivation in P(MOCA)

Ideally, internal motivation grows out of our highest, most hopeful needs rather than fears, ego, or greed.

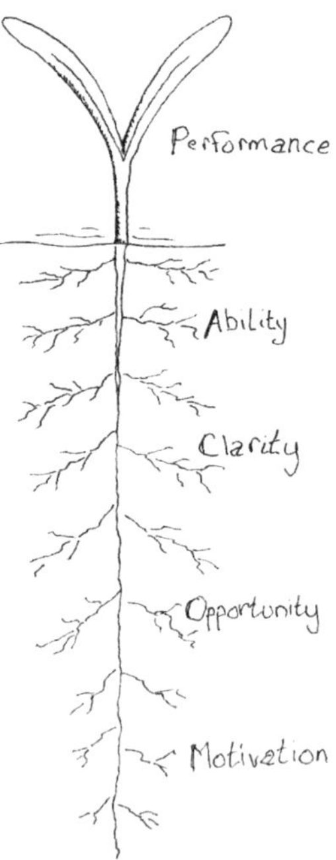

One way to visualize the idea of P(MOCA) is as a root system that produces a growing, fruitful plant of motivation and performance.

As we try a new task, we are motivated to perform by our desire to develop and prove we have the **ability** to do the work. This source of motivation works well for the first few times we try something new, but it quickly fades after a success or two. Leaders can support early successes by ensuring people in new roles have everything they need to demonstrate their ability to succeed. This establishes a pattern of completed dopamine loops from the start, which creates strong internal motivations.

After we know we can do a task, we get interested in **clarity**– figuring out how to do it better, more completely, and precisely. This source of motivation may last a few hours or even a few months depending on the complexity of the task.

A leader's most energizing role is creating clarity of expectations around processes and outcomes for new team members. You can likely recall a surge of motivation to act once someone took the time to explain exactly how you could help.

Next, **opportunity** will naturally become our driving force as we seek to reduce the amount of time it takes to complete a task. Once we gain speed, we will want to experiment with our ability to exercise authority to find more creative and personally satisfying ways to do the work. This source can fuel our internal motivation for years.

If we're exploring and exercising our choice, freedom, and self determination, we will build our personal initiative, confidence, and self esteem. That practice will get us through a lot of hard times and discouragement. If the role does not allow for some creativity, motivated workers will often seek a new role once they can see the dead end clearly.

Now things get interesting and a bit edgy. In our roots image our deepest source of **motivation** is the exploration of the **source** of motivation itself. In the practice of self inquiry– being curious, humble, and experimental with ourselves– we may discover our most durable and sustaining sources of motivation as I did with my needs for authorship and freedom.

If we're motivated by self authority and self exploration as paths towards understanding what it means to be human, we're working from a very personal, durable foundation. This place of empowerment reinforces our sense of the world as a dynamic place to explore, grow and express ourselves, rather than a threatening place where we have to prove, defend, and protect ourselves. We don't always have a choice, but if we can arrange it, most of us would choose the more positive option.

These personal motivations can turn even "simple" tasks into paths toward personal experimentation and expression, as when Brother Lawrence cooked as a form of prayer in Paris, or a Zen monk carries water and chops wood as a spiritual exercise. When we live in self authority and intentional attention, we begin to accept our own and other's most elemental states of being. "This is who and how I am, here, now." In exchange, we can gain a lifetime of clarity, learning, wisdom and compassion.

How do some people persevere better than others? How do they master skills and domains over many years? They must be sourcing their motivation differently from most of us who wrestle with willpower and self discipline.

We want to find a durable source of motivation that allows us to persevere through hard times. It gives us what Angela Duckworth calls "grit" in her book of that title. Reaching further back, Nietzsche calls perseverance "long obedience in the same direction" in *Beyond Good and Evil.*

Of course, motivation is a continuous dance between shallowest and deepest, internal and external, between checklists and hope, deadlines and faith. Unfortunately, many people dance in a very narrow, fearful range at the top of the roots. With shallow roots, their motivation often withers without daily watering from small wins and encouragement. Of course, really great performers capable of taking on large strategic projects must survive long periods of heat and drought without withering. They must tap their most sustainably inspiring root system of motivations.

Ontological Roots of Motivation

The deepest, strongest, most enduring roots of our motivation rest on a core ontological question: What kind of human am I?

Let's look at our motivational root system another way. First, let's define terms. Ontology relates to our state of being (I am good, so I did X) while teleology relates to the ends justifying the means (money is good, so I did X).

We can work out of ontological, or "Who am I" questions every day. Am I:

- Effective or inert?
- A giver or a taker?
- Hopeful or cynical?
- Faithful or expedient?

If I am committed to living my life as an effective giver who works with hope and faith to actualize these values, to be the change I want to see in the world, I will have more durable, stronger sources of motivation than a person who impulsively lives off the fat of the land in cynical convenience.

Choosing to act out of hope is the heart of humane leadership.

I assume you are a hopeful, humane leader.

Through this lens, we'll use the same plant image to look at the roots of performance and motivation.

The leaves of performance grow atop a root system of deepening motivations with different descriptions. At the shallowest level, we are motivated by impulse: "I feel like it, I do it." Lower down, our mind engages with our willpower and makes plans. As we move deeper, inspiration underpins our plans. Most profound of all lie our hopes for who we might be and our faith in living our destiny and values.

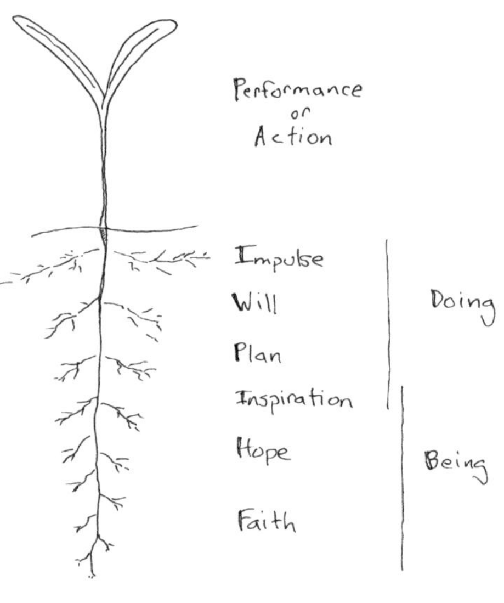

Entry level workers may sing, "I owe, I owe, it's off to work I go" while a founder of a biotech startup might be living out hopes to be a person who helps cure a form of cancer. Entry level people may start work from an impulse to earn money and a will to avoid poverty while the most successful entrepreneurs can work for years from their hopes and faith in themselves and their visions.

At this deepest level, we aspire to be a person using our unique strengths and opportunities to meaningfully serve as many as possible. You may seek to heal the sick, feed the hungry, or inspire millions with your art while I seek to empower leaders to enlighten and ennoble their work. When we're an aspirant, discouragement, negative feedback, or short term failures are just part of a much longer and very important game.

A person motivated by firmly rooted aspirations might say, "I was born to be a great architect, people just haven't recognized the truth yet." The Smithsonian magazine described American architect Frank Lloyd Wright as having, "unshakable optimism, messianic zeal and pragmatic resilience." People who have faith in their destiny are not easily discouraged, they say, "No, this is just a part of my path. I will keep going."

Many artists have worked all their lives with no recognition or encouragement, but they kept working because their motivation was rooted in a faith in their ontological sense of destiny. It may look like will power to people working from shallower motivations, but when pressed, the artist will often speak in terms of passion, not having any choice, or ontological destiny.

Lived Values

From whence does this sense of who we are meant to be arise?

Philosophers have wrestled with ontological questions for thousands of years without finding a solid answer. It's possible that when we realize we have no choice but to live out our values we reach this profound spring of motivation.

> Be the change you wish to see in the world.
>
> — Arleen Lorrance

For years I tried to live other people's values, choosing to follow the flash of opportunity, the demands of a role, and the needs of my clients. One day in the desert I realized I no longer had any choice. I was no longer able to convince myself to override my values– the humane leadership values outlined in chapter one.

Shared, lived values form the social contract at the heart of any team or relationship. How can you trust a person who might lack courage and strength, who might not be balanced, fair, wise, or caring in a crucial moment?

Living these values converts them into the virtues that define our character, our leadership, and the culture of our organizations. We seek to be living examples, exemplum. I developed these tools and methods because as a non-functionally introverted young person, I needed them. I still work with them daily, personally and with clients. Using these tools, I have been able to discover ways to live my own values, and now, to help you and as you become a living example of yours.

In your daily experiments, you will notice that we motivate ourselves from sources up and down the continuum. Sometimes we are smoothly moving towards our goals, checking things off the list; "Edit chapter, build new web page, meet with a prospect." We can work at the shallower levels of motivation, Will and Plan. But if we run into a serious setback, we may need to dip into Hope and Faith to keep ourselves moving. We may say to ourselves, "Am I going to be a quitter? Or, am I going to be a person who pursues great things in this life even on hard days?"

In the end, I hope that you will become an exemplum and a giver of encouragement and generative care to those around you as you invite them to live their values.

Our goal is to use this admittedly idealized model to experiment with sources of motivation that will sustain our long obedience to our values.

You have everything you need to be an excellent, humane leader. I look forward to hearing about what you learn along the way.

Further reading

- "Eastern Needs More Than a New Image to Win Back Friends and Customers," Sun-Sentinel, 1991
- Dickens, *Hard Times*, 1854
- Forester, "The Other Side of the Hedge," available free online
- Lubow, "The Triumph of Frank Lloyd Wright," Smithsonian, June 2009
- Semler, interviewed by Tim Ferris, #229 on Tim.blog

8

If we are leaders of our own organizations, we have a great deal of control and responsibility for choosing appropriate, effective external motivations. If we are in a large organization as a leader, we must know exactly what the organization is incentivizing, both officially and unofficially. We cannot be humane leaders and also accept the traditional teleological, manipulative culture of external motivation.

Recently there were headlines in the business press about our next bosses being algorithms. I believe that anyone with an incentive plan is already reporting to an algorithm. Unfortunately, most of the algorithms in place today are imprecise if not precisely wrong.

Our humane leadership values of fair strength, wise balance and generative care allow us to experience humane leadership as both heartful and accountable at once. Let's explore how to build real accountability into our team's work.

Accountable to MBO, OKRs and KPIs?

Accountability for results is a keystone of modern leadership. The promise of scientific management, starting with Frederick Taylor, was "whatever you can measure, you can manage." We seek to measure work and results via popular structures like management by objective (MBO), objectives and key results (OKR) or key performance indicators (KPI).

Unfortunately, many humane leaders are trying to hold personal connection, optimism, and faith in the face of often unrealistic and erroneous measures of success / performance.

Are we tempted to set unrealistic goals based on inaccurate operating metaphors? If we think of our organizations as machines to be optimized, we are tempted to think of the humans on our teams as interchangeable parts. If we wear one out by running the machine too fast, what does that cost us? What are the assumptions about humans built into the metaphors you use? Watch Frontline's documentary, "Amazon Empire" to see the challenges clearly.

To work from our humane leadership values and to hold people accountable, we need to create realistic performance goals. Realistic performance goals are a key driver of employee experience, work life balance, employee engagement, and turnover.

Performance Goals and Work Life Balance
Gallup, 10/2019

<table>
<tr><td colspan="2" rowspan="2"></td><td colspan="2">Boss sets realistic performance goals</td></tr>
<tr><td>Strongly agree</td><td>Do not agree</td></tr>
<tr><td rowspan="2">I can maintain work life balance</td><td>Strongly agree</td><td>64%</td><td>26%</td></tr>
<tr><td>Do not agree</td><td>36%</td><td>74%</td></tr>
</table>

Realistic goals contribute to work life balance, unrealistic goals destroy balance.

MBO (management by objective) is a management model that aims to improve performance by clearly defining objectives that are agreed to by both management and employees. "Stretch goals"and "big hairy audacious goals" are wonderful if we choose them for ourselves, like "Let's see if we can build this barn in one day" or "Can we hike 20 miles today?" But does your team really have a choice or are their metrics derived from financial targets handed down from above? We might find ourselves saying, "Headquarters is asking for 10% year over year growth," "They asked us to cut another 10% from unit cost," or "Our labor budget has been cut 20%."

The question is who chose the goal and why? This leads to exploring our possible sources of motivation:

- Joy of trying.
- Proving something to yourself or someone else.
- Keeping our jobs.
- Proving we have power over others.
- Mechanistic pursuit of some self-serving outcomes.
- The grand refutation of your deepest fears.
- Manipulation for fun or profit.

As humane leaders, we need to be very clear about the motivational source of our goals before we ask ourselves or others to sign up to reach for them. Our goals should be engaging, focusing, and supportive of healthy work life balance for our team members. A good goal will support concentrated, transcendent flow states, but won't push us to harm ourselves in the short or long terms.

> First, do no harm.
>
> — Hippocrates

MBO is great in theory but many objectives do not have clear causal chains leading to success, especially if you are working in a complex, adaptive environment. Many OKRs or KPIs that rely on human (especially customer) actions, like sales goals, are only loosely coupled causal chains. Humans are the epitome of complex adaptive systems. How can we hold a person on our team accountable for many other people's actions they only influence but never control?

My experience is that MBO in practice is too often high-level executives setting arbitrary financial goals which then roll down into MBO targets for sales or operating efficiencies. They essentially say to their subordinates, "Here's the goal. Even though we don't understand it ourselves, and no one else has ever figured it out, we pay you to do this, so we'll pay you a bonus if you can make it work. Go!"

Aspirational goals can be useful forcing functions to drive innovation. But stretch goals can become demoralizing to those who must hit the target to earn meaningful incentive pay. Some causal chains will defy our understanding. But, humane leaders can partner with their teams to consciously, creatively experiment with uncovering the real causal chains that lead to the results they want. The key is trying to hold the team's motivation, healthy balance, and cohesion when the MBO incentives prove elusive.

Ideally, before creating goals, incentives, and accountability structures, we as leaders need to be very clear about how value is created:

- Causal chains
- Correlations of effort and result
- Controllable and uncontrollable variables

Sounds good, but how can a leader figure this all out?

Mapping the Organization Algorithm

In order to create a useful, evolving map of causal chains, it's helpful to think of an organization as a nested set of algorithms in which there are constants, variables, operations, processes, and results. The leader's job is to understand all the value creation variables and how they relate to each other so results are efficiently and predictably reached. Frontline people are unlikely to be able to see the map of all these nested algorithms, but those people are a rich source of understanding about their piece of the equation and its many critical inputs.

For instance, a product design algorithm might take in inputs around customer needs and preferences, production capabilities, demand, evaluation of certain needs being fulfilled, all kinds of market and engineering data, and then bring it into a process like a modern product development process– for instance an agile, iterative process– or it could be an old school, waterfall design specification process. Out will come a new product to offer: the product design algorithm's output.

If you're going to produce a physical product, you're going to have material inputs, a bill of materials, all kinds of tools and processes, labor, and training on how to produce this thing, and then you're going to have a set of inventory coming out the back end. Hopefully one of the inputs will be some projections of demand, and you'll be able to forecast how many you should make for this first batch. The production algorithm will result in inventory to sell.

That new product in inventory will then feed into the marketing and sales processes, and those teams will do their best to tell the story, find prospects and close deals. Any error in the product design or production algorithms will feed into and hinder the marketing and sales results. Marketing and sales algorithms are normally more difficult to figure out because they involve the greatest of all variables: humans trying to influence the behavior of other humans.

Nested algorithms, like our firms themselves, are complex. For curious leaders, these nested algorithms are an intriguing and rewarding puzzle. When I was deep in operations, I looked into what was going wrong with deliveries and what we could do about it. To make it interesting for myself and to identify the variables that I could affect, I got philosophical and scientific about the work that needed to be done.

I started mapping the processes that fed the delivery system and the shipping system. A load of shipments required a plan by my team and a set of shipping labels with related greeting cards and appropriate products for each shipment. I started mapping all these elements as potential error sources using Unified Modeling Language practices to create a dependency tree.

To explore just one element of a shipment, **product,** let's look at the potential error sources. Correct product on the shipping dock for a planned load required a warehouse pull request. The pull request required complete, accurate data in the inventory management system. That required regular quality assurance inspections, accurate inventory counts, location, and production batch data. That required forklift drivers using their scanners and inventory movement processes correctly. Production batch data required accurate bills of materials and product information management system data, which required accurate and timely data in the production planning and control systems and processes. That required that the information technology department databases were properly built and data governance rules were in place and followed.

In any business, the leg bone is connected to the hip bone and someone needs to understand how it all fits together both ideally and in reality. Not to mention what might go wrong along the way. This clarity was my unique, relevant contribution.

My dependency tree started with a successful delivery of top-quality product. This successful outcome depended upon having the correct product arrive on time at the correct address with the correct greeting card. The correct product arriving on time depended upon having the carrier deliver as expected (no weather events, accidents, or parades along the route), a good address, the customer checking their mailbox or door step before a sticky-fingered neighbor did, etc. The correct address depended upon our address entry rules and the recipient address entered by the customer. On and on these dependency trees branched back into product information creation, packaging design, online ordering applications, the customer-facing website, so on and so forth.

I built this dependency tree and the potential error sources they represented by leaving my desk and visiting all the people doing the actual work. In the refrigerated cold storage rooms, forklift drivers told me how mislabeled pallets led to packages missing their intended trucks. Career fruit inspectors explained how fruit procurement decisions to use cheap, slow inbound freight carriers sometimes led to low quality fruit that required express shipment to avoid spoilage.

Inventory data managers told me all the ways our system created complexity around the creation of accurate bills of materials. Merchants explained all the ways their production planning could miss demand, leaving us with backorders. IT techs showed me how custom greeting cards could be mixed up, miscut and detached from their ticket batch and shipping appointment. I mapped scores of error sources across all the departments and process flows of the organization.

I ended up with a two foot by three foot map of the processes, error sources and the business units responsible across the entire organization all the way back to root causes in design, process and data.

I love research, so I had a lot of fun developing that error source map. The job became much more interesting when I was not just reacting to errors but actually finding their root causes. It also put me in a position to quickly visualize the source of errors being discussed in meetings and solve problems quickly, or avoid them before they happened. As I was fond of saying at the time, the person who sweeps up after the parade has a unique insight into the health of the elephants. I learned a lot of messy but very valuable realities of the business in this process.

Digging into the nested algorithms of an organization is like developing a superpower for making an impact and earning influence across and at higher levels of the organization. It also tells you exactly which measures will create real value in your organization.

If the leader is not going to do this work, who will? Leaders can't rely on frontline people to do this analysis, but the frontline people often possess invaluable understanding of certain variables and parts of the causal chains. The leader becomes the student, analyst, synthesizer, and librarian of the realities of the processes and earns more influence in the organization with each new insight gained.

Later, when my map helped earn me a role running the business sales division, I could see the squishy assumptions and arbitrary nature of the percentage growth sales goals I was assigned. It was clear there were far more variables contributing to our sales than anyone was considering when setting the goals.

In this new position, I negotiated for realistic numbers, but in the end, the board had a vision and the C-suite did their best to temper that vision with reality. I set out to learn the business sale causal chain and figured out not only how product design and messaging influenced sales but also how the best sales people guided sales conversations and how many conversations they could have per hour.

In my search for root causes, I became curious about why our customers gifted in the first place. What was the process in a person's mind that caused them to want to send a gift to another human they do business with – to their client, their referral source, or their associates?

I dug into the psychology of gifting and came across, Robert Cialdini's, *Influence: The Psychology of Persuasion,* and found a crucial idea, the norm of reciprocity. Understanding the norm of reciprocity revealed the powerful algorithm underlying business gifting.

This linkage is so powerful, in the fields of finance, medicine, and government gifting is severely restricted by industry specific rules (e.g. FINRA Rule 3220 and ACA section 6002 Physician Payment Sunshine Act). When I understood the power of the social psychology of the norm of reciprocity, suddenly these restrictions on gifting made sense; an unreciprocated gift is a very powerful tool for manipulating other people's behavior.

This insight into the norm of reciprocity made our selling much easier in unregulated industries, because we could educate prospects on the norm of reciprocity. We could now say, "Here's a tool that's so effective it has to be regulated in some industries. You're not in a regulated industry, why aren't you gifting to build business relationships?" This insight clarified the value proposition and the calculus in people's minds, changing the way we unfolded our sales conversations and which industries we addressed. For instance, we put less energy into the financial industry because we knew it was so restricted, but focused on businesses more free to gift.

This deep learning is fascinating work. It is the opportunity and responsibility of the leader to drive research into how performance is affected positively and negatively by all of these variables and error sources. Once you know the variables, then you can start experimenting with affecting them, and better evaluate and incentivize your team's success in reaching your goals. This learning about the variables, causal chains and nested algorithms of your organization becomes the foundation for your ability to externally motivate others and earn influence for yourself.

The Variables That Count

Assuming you really do want to understand how your team creates value, once you have a basic map of your organization's algorithms, it's important to understand which variables are independent (not controlled by other variables in our algorithm) and which are dependent (controllable by variables we can influence). Understanding the nature of the variables that drive the results we seek allows us to focus our efforts and incentives effectively.

Understanding the nature of our variables also helps us maintain our mental health.

> Grant me the serenity
> To accept the things I cannot change;
> Courage to change the things I can;
> And wisdom to know the difference.
>
> — Reinhold Neibuhr

We must focus our team's efforts and incentives on the variables they **can** control.

For instance in sales work, there are two important dependent variables:

- **Quantity of sales effort**– how many texts, emails or phone calls are going out? These are dependent on a person's Motivation and Opportunity.
- **Quality of the sales effort**– the ability of the salesperson, the quality of the offering, messaging, scripts,

landing pages, calls to action, etc. This is dependent on the Clarity of Expectations and Ability.

If we hold the right person accountable for the right variables, we invite focused work and learning towards our goals. We can control the quantity of human efforts to reach out, we can control the quality of the value proposition, the messaging and sales team training.

The P(MOCA) model makes human performance a more dependent (controllable) variable in the algorithm of your organization.

But, we cannot control a sales result because we cannot control the client's decision to buy today, that's an independent variable. Our efforts might influence their decision, but we can't control their purchase in a free society.

If we set up well-designed experiments on the dependent variables in our organization's algorithm, then it becomes possible to hold people accountable in a humane way. With data to back us up, it's easy to then ask salespeople struggling to perform:

- How many times did you dial the phone, send SMS or email today?
- Did you follow the directions in terms of targeting people appropriately?
- Did you deliver the message as we trained you to?
- Were you responsive to people's questions?

- Were you curious? What did you learn about these clients?
- How quickly were you able to qualify them as prospects?

This is a far more informative and supportive conversation than the old, Glengarry Glen Ross style sales review meeting that was more like, "Did you hit your sales goal? What are you going to do about it?" Focusing on results misses the opportunity to learn how to improve outcomes.

If we hold accountability on the wrong person/variable combinations, we will link rewards to events the person did not control. Rewarding blind luck wastes money and discourages the team members who were trying hard but weren't lucky this time. Either way, we run afoul of the law of unintended consequences and create counterproductive and aberrant behavior.

For instance, in colonial India, There was a problem with cobras biting people. The British authorities offered a reward for every dead cobra delivered in Delhi. People started killing all the dangerous snakes they could find. Things got better. Some enterprising locals started breeding more cobras so they could collect more rewards. As soon as the British authorities learned that their rewards were creating this counterproductive behavior, they immediately stopped paying. The many breeders turned their suddenly worthless cobras loose on the streets where they began multiplying rapidly. Things got worse.

Unintended Consequences: Software Sales Measures

For a modern example of unintended consequences in business we can look at many outwardly successful sales organizations. I recently consulted with a software vendor who'd built a multi-billion dollar global business by incenting their sales teams to meet quarterly sales goals by product and market (independent variables). The sales team dutifully focused on delivering revenue to drive quarterly results to impress analysts and investors, the stock price went up, everyone cheered.

It all looked like a huge win until we talked with the marketing team and their external strategic implementation partners (IT consulting firms). The marketing team could see that the brand was increasingly seen as an expensive, low-return investment. The strategic partners stopped inviting the vendor's salespeople to client meetings because they were so focused on the sale this quarter that they tended to miss or short circuit much larger strategic opportunities. For clients, because many of the software modules sold proved really complex to implement and only marginally beneficial to the end user, they became shelfware (software owned by IT but never used in the business). As a result, the brand, the strategic partners and the clients all suffered unintended consequences. Because of the focus on quarterly results, management never gained the courage to disconnect sales compensation from quarterly product sales goals. The company is still seen as a success, yet operates far below its full market potential, embitters customers, and competes with faster growing competitors.

Another enterprise software firm with a cloud-based platform focuses their team's compensation on monthly customer consumed services measures. These are tied to direct client value because cloud services can be turned on and off by the client. This business and compensation model aligns team effort and incentives with client value created by services used. Everyone wins in their simple, transparent model that focuses on monthly client perceived value rather than large upfront sales numbers pushed on a quarterly basis.

In the "sell big packages aggressively" model, short term success sowed the seeds for long term challenges around client value, brand, strategic partnerships and even sales talent turnover. The best salespeople chose to escape the demoralizing grind to hit goals they could only influence but not control.

In the end, humane leaders seek to understand and work from dependent variables. This alignment gives our teams a deep sense of motivation based in clarity about what's controllable and what's not.

Designing Living Incentives

Often, we design incentives around the easily measured outcomes the organization desires (the scoreboard) instead of the winning actions that lead to positive results (how we play the game).

A more humane framework for designing incentives returns to the roots of motivation. Incentives should be tied to behaviors the person can control and the positive experiences they can gain by contributing to the organization's goals.

Returning to our roots of motivation image, we can see that for team members just starting in new roles, incentives (like earning their place on the team) related to proving **ability** and **clarity** are most important. This idea is built into a traditional apprenticeship or probationary period.

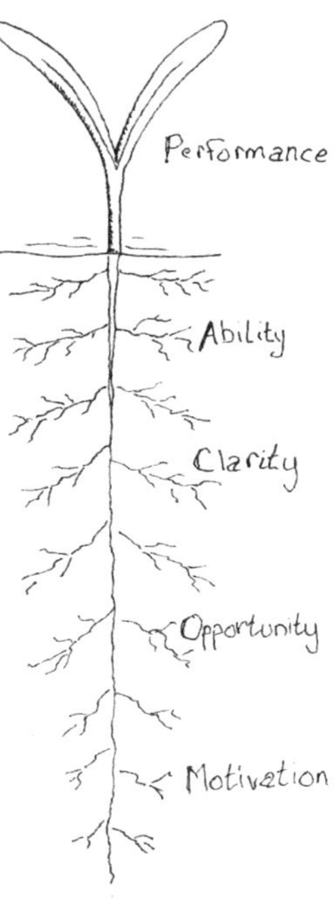

Once firmly rooted as a capable member of the team, the person's incentives can be designed around expanding **opportunities** to contribute, including the freedom to go faster and assume more personal authority that can lead to earning a bonus or commission for hitting stretch performance goals. Or, in Brazil, Ricardo Semler focuses incentives on time and smooth operations, so when his sales people reach their revenue target for the week, they can take the rest of the week off at full pay.

Finally, at the deepest levels, we are **motivated** to control our contributions to our own growth, impact and income. These are typically executive-level bonuses for designing and delivering long-term strategic outcomes.

Leaders must design incentives appropriate to the person's stage of career and sources of motivation. Once a person has figured out how to do a job well, large commissions may motivate them to work more quickly and consistently. But large commissions may be wasted on an employee seeking deeper, longer-term sources of motivation for creative expression and strategic successes.

Loose, Tight, Agile and Balance

To engage our team's full humanity with all of its possibilities and failings, we need to have an appropriate mix of freedom and accountability.

We love the experience of liberty that looseness gives us. Some of us are motivated by our love of a blank piece of paper and the freedom of time to fill it, a great question or a tough problem. These humans are often the ones who are quite innovative and productive of new and interesting things; the artists and inventors. Nearly every organization wants to attract more creative people like these. But how can we balance that liberty with accountability?

Internal motivations are linked to our sense of freedom while accountability helps incorporate external motivations. It's unhealthy to have freedom without responsibility or to be internally focused without acknowledging the needs of others. A living, sustainable motivation is a dance between internal and external motivators, needs, constraints and forcing functions.

In fact, in the 1970's there was a move to build a Statue of Responsibility in San Francisco Bay to balance the Statue of Liberty in New York Harbor.

How can we create a balance of freedom and accountability for ourselves and others?

Chunking

A precursor of work satisfaction and accountability is designing satisfying chunks of work. In some manufacturing jobs a piece rate leads to the dopamine hit of quick completion before starting on the next piece.

In work that takes longer to complete, leaders must work with their team members to design chunks of a focusing, rewarding, and challenging size. This creates discrete, understandable tasks with milestones achievable in a half or full day. Clarity creates motivation and focus and the end point becomes a mini success. The tempo of completing a task or milestone can be punctuated by regular micro celebrations. Each of these small but meaningful celebrations builds motivation and momentum towards the goal.

Over the last few days, my motivation was low as I worked on this book. I realized that I was taking too long to close the dopamine loops when transcribing my paper edits into digital documents. Noticing this, I shortened up the time in between my hand edits and typing. This simple re-chunking improved my engagement, satisfaction, and productivity tremendously.

Time-Based Forcing Functions

Next, we can create time-based forcing functions for ourselves. Our monochronic model of time, this happens, then that happens, allows us to sequence and accelerate complex sequences of work in projects. Forcing functions are "behavior shaping constraints" in time. For example, our decision to pull off the freeway might be forced by the ages of the passengers, bladder capacity, and time since our last stop.

Leaders design forcing functions to drive performance. "Great, I will set a meeting tomorrow morning to review your work." Experiment with designing forcing functions for yourself and others. Personally, I'm experimenting with creating forcing functions by setting client meetings to prepare for, workshops to deliver, and public speaking dates that force me to create and refine content.

But how much of this tightness and drive can a team take? How do we gauge the well-being of the team and the quality of the work if we are running too tight or have too many forcing functions? Commonly defined "effective" leaders learn to use forcing functions and become addicted, as project management becomes the great savior and then tormentor of organization.

Collaborative Forcing Functions: Agile

To find a balance, we can adopt collaborative, self-regulating social forcing functions. This starts to blend the monochronic approach with the polychronic, more integrated, and organic approach to time and human relations.

Agile uses intense periods of self-organizing work toward a milestone to balance loose-tight approaches. It does this by freeing the team to structure its own work and create its own social accountability and motivations around time-limited sprints. Projects are broken into logical chunks worked on in sprints with daily standup meetings to close risk-mitigating feedback loops for the team. This works well in software engineering and any other collaborative, creative work that requires more than a few days to complete.

Agile daily standup meetings ensure that expectations are clarified regularly and ability issues are surfaced and supported before they create problems. Performance is improved, pace is accelerated, and flexibility is maximized.

In Amsterdam, Taco Dibbits, Director of the Rijksmuseum wanted to reset the museum to showcase more of the collection and engage visitors in an innovative way. He said, "In Dutch, we say, 'Let everybody fly.' But as leaders, we also have to let our teams know where they are flying to; otherwise there's a risk they will become frustrated and deflated. I think agile leaders need to understand that for teams to self organize and self direct, they also need to have a very clear and thoughtfully constrained task."

I am happy to report that we found the results of the Rjiksmuseum's innovative efforts fresh, engaging and stunningly beautiful.

Even though we love freedom, people work best within clear constraints. We need structure and tightness to feel productive, but we can easily forget to give ourselves and each other freedom to breathe, create and celebrate. It's about a playful, living balance of loose and tight. Agile methodologies seem to offer the best dance of freedom and accountability, internal and external motivations we've seen to date.

Looseness

The fourth type of experiment we can run is building in looseness. Build in time each day to walk, to stretch, to breathe in and out. Mindfulness practices, four-day work weeks, off-sites, and sabbaticals are all experiments with looseness being run by progressive organizations today. A caveat; do these practices deepen our awareness of our own sources of motivation or are we using them as bandages on the wounds inflicted by an organization addicted to external, fear-based motivations?

Some firms are experimenting with allowing staff to dedicate 10% of their work time to personally chosen intrapreneur projects aligned with the goals of the organization. 3M has offered these creative hours for years. Financial software firm Intuit even hosts idea incubation and presentation events, contests, and internal venture capital programs to turn staff freedom into client-facing product and service innovations.

How can you balance your own needs for freedom and structure? Is there a tempo of movement from loose to tight that works better for you? How do your needs for loose and tight shift during the day or week? Can you roll the ideas that work for you into your organization?

Humane leaders will see loose and tight experiments as important opportunities to learn and innovate in their personal and professional lives. Understanding of the needs of each individual in our care and the variables they can control in creating value for clients and the organization will increase engagement and productivity while tapping into the steady power of deeply rooted, internal motivations.

Further reading

- Cialdini, Influence: *The Psychology of Persuasion*, 1984
- Csikszentmihalyi, *Flow: The Psychology of Optimal Experience*, 1990
- Gallup, "Do Your Managers Know How to Improve Work-Life Balance?" October, 2019
- Lean Manufacturing Practices– many good resources online
- Mamet, *Glengarry Glen Ross*, 1983
- Merton, *The Unanticipated Consequences of Purposive Social Action*, 1936

9

In our humane model of performance, opportunity is about giving team members the authority and time to perform well. Leaders help their teams manage obstacles, scarcity of time, and perceived limits to their authority.

In my experience, empowering and enabling people to engage with new opportunities is a great joy. Often real growth only requires the leader's invitation to try.

> If you have some power, then your job is to empower somebody else.
>
> — Toni Morrison

We see opportunities as precious, time-bound assets that call for careful stewardship. It is up to leaders to match opportunities with a person's potential for contribution and growth.

Of course we want to avoid missing a precious opportunity altogether by assigning someone who is not able or motivated to seize it. At the same time, why waste an opportunity to enable and encourage a team member by assigning it to someone who has done it a thousand times already and will not be stretched by the experience?

When looking at their organizations and the value they create, humane leaders don't see people sitting in chairs fulfilling roles, they see a set of opportunities placed before people who are each striving to grow themselves and the organization.

- Are the people on your team challenged and engaged or stifled and bored?
- Are the people, their ability to contribute, and the value they create **growing**?

We naturally look at ourselves first to see if we are opening and expanding our own opportunities in creative and conscious ways. Have we designed our own portfolio of opportunities to be:

- Engaging?
- Challenging?
- Empowering?

Foundations of Authority

Opportunities require some authority– the power to decide what work will be done by whom, when, and how– to pursue them.

We may use our authority to take action ourselves or delegate work to others. Either way, we need the power to decide. Authority, according to Betrand Russell in Power: A New Social Analysis, comes in three forms:

- Force / coercion
- Inducements / incentives / bribes
- Propaganda / persuasion / influence / habit

Building on Russell's ideas in the late 1950s, social psychologists French and Raven laid out six foundations of power:

- **Coercive**– the leader can punish those who don't follow. This has negative long term impacts on everyone involved, so please keep reading this list to find sources of power that will serve you.
- **Legitimate**– the leader has an assigned, role-based right to ask for compliance and obedience. Ideally, we earn our legitimate influence by being relevant, unique and visible. Of course, leaders can be assigned a leadership role, but only earned influence will allow the person to legitimately lead via persuasion over the long run. "Because I said so," "Do it or else," and "Don't you want the bonus?" are phrases that signal the failure of a leader to earn internally motivated habitual high performance from their team.
- **Referent**– the leader seems worthy of obedience given their qualities of character, size, and / or dashing good looks. Consider taking on some of the pretenses of leadership to allow others to align comfortably with

your influence and authority. So, dress for your next role, act with clarity, confidence and commitment while still aspiring to earn influence with the next three foundations.

- **Informational**– the leader offers or controls the information required for the team to succeed. We aspire to be relevant by providing unique insights and data rather than constricting the flow of information as a means of gaining power.
- **Expert**– the leader gains influence with relevant skills and knowledge. This is the heart of our aspirations to be competent, to earn influence by being a font of relevant experience and wisdom.
- **Reward**– the leader can offer incentives to followers. Unfortunately, rewards can be twisted into bribery that demeans everyone involved. Bribery can be outright criminal or simply taking a paycheck for work you care little about. Humane leaders offer us our own experience of contributing to the world, beyond our vision of what's possible. An expanded sense of self is the greatest reward we can offer one another.

Humane leaders understand each of these bases of power, and are not afraid to occasionally and deftly use less enlightened sources of power like legitimate and coercive tools to protect the health and performance of the team in critical moments. But we want to minimize our use of force, bribery, and rewards to get things done because these are external, fear, or greed-based motivations that sow the seeds of their own eventual ineffectiveness.

Leadership & Consent

With today's most skilled workers, any shred of unearned or non-consensual authority will almost inevitably lead to disengagement, underperformance and turnover. Usually your very best performers have the most options and the least patience for poor leadership. Poor leadership can quickly leave you with only your most resigned, least qualified team members struggling to meet minimum performance standards.

The right to lead is distinct from the assigned role and is earned in the process of daily interactions. How can leaders earn the consent to legitimately influence their team?

- **Be curious** about what's relevant to the individuals on the team
- **Be clear** about performance and behavior expectations for the team
- **Be cautious and courageous** at once by making a few promises that can absolutely be kept
- **Be conscious** that every day is a fresh opportunity to earn more influence with the team.

These simple steps are a good start, but let's dig more deeply into the daily work of earning influence.

Earning Influence

After reading Bertrand Russell's book on power as a young man, I actively sought responsibility and the authority that came with it. I figured someone had to lead and I didn't much like how most people in power behaved. I assumed that opportunities were opened by actively pursuing them. In the process of reading Russell's book, I realized that earning influence relied on three variables.

Earned Influence = Relevant * Unique * Visible

or, written as a function, P(R,U,V)

Essentially, power is a function of creating what's relevant to other people, finding opportunities for impact that might not occur to everyone else, and making your work publicly visible and accessible. This, like the MOCA model, became an idea that shaped my daily actions almost every day afterwards. It's a powerful model because it works across any set of humans– from global enterprise leadership teams to local arts organizations, even to families.

Earning Influence Story: Erica & The Film Festival

Erica is a talented young woman with a fantastic opportunity to become the operational leader of a regional film festival, but some worry she might be too young for the job.

When I started advising Erica, the first mental model I taught her was this earned influence model. As I saw it, her challenge was to earn influence with her peers on staff, the executive director and the board of directors. But, how would she find what was most relevant?

After the departure of the prior, very experienced operations manager, Erica quickly realized that in the first year, smooth, stable execution of operations were at risk and was therefore the most relevant accomplishment she could produce. If she could increase festival revenues as well, that would be great. She was in a unique position as operations manager to contribute to those goals.

As a part of her work in the first year, she made a courageous choice, after consulting with key stakeholders, to change the ticketing system for the festival. She chose to take on this unique, relevant contribution with her new systems administrator who was also looking for an opportunity to make her mark by modernizing the organization's guest experience. Erica organized the work of evaluating, gaining board approval, negotiating the terms, and supporting the conversion process to the new system. The system was a huge improvement, and the project greatly enhanced Erica's earned influence with the staff, the board of directors, and with the leading software vendor in the industry.

In parallel to the ticketing system project, Erica was invited to attend an industry association meeting. After making unique and relevant contributions in peer discussions, she was asked to serve on a discussion panel and later to serve on the association's board of directors.

In her late twenties, Erica is building her earned influence on local and national levels. Now she's working methodically to earn the influence required to take over the Executive Director role from her current boss who would love to focus on the Artistic Director role. It's wonderful when an enlightened leader creates an opening for an emerging one. But what about bigger, more competitive work environments?

This process of earning influence works especially well in more complex organizations because they offer more opportunities to cross silos, levels, and existing social structures to bring unique solutions to relevant problems.

Extending relevance

To extend your relevance in a larger organization, look beyond your current place in the power structure. Respect, but do not feel limited by your existing role, existing silos, and the chain of command in your organization.

Every organization suffers from siloization, so you can often be relevant and unique simply by crossing them. The goal is to understand what's relevant to more people– especially those with influence– within your organization and beyond.

- What are their goals, performance measures, and deliverables?
- How could you and your team support their goals?
- What's being lost in your siloed organization?
- How can you eliminate any friction or blockage?

When you list these various sets of goals and measures, you will begin to see overlaps between other's goals, your goals, and your relevant skills and capabilities. It may make sense to make a Venn diagram to help yourself visualize the shared goals. As you discover them, develop relationships with the people who share your goals. That can be as simple as inviting them for a quick sync meeting. I would suggest these meetings by saying, "I want to be sure my department is in sync with your needs and goals. Can we meet for 15 minutes to start the discussion?" Out of those conversations come opportunities to collaborate where values, challenges, and goals align.

Discovering Relevance

The easy way to be relevant is to **ask.**

Most people never ask and even fewer listen to the needs expressed when people are speaking. Anyone can become more relevant simply by asking, listening, clarifying, and then acting on the needs of others.

Questions honestly and compassionately asked are often a gift to the person we ask. Questions can set us free from misunderstandings, worries, and many similar torments.

Asking good questions and actually listening to the answers bridges us into the heart of relevance to others.

People will often answer an honest, present question with exactly what they want and need, exactly what is most relevant to them. It's a gift to ask a good question and the answer you receive may be a gift back to you. Practice asking better, more relevant questions, it serves everyone involved because the quality of our lives is often defined by the quality of the questions we ask.

Excellent resources for asking better questions are: David Whyte in conversation with Krista Tippett (see the further reading list at the end of this chapter on what they call, "beautiful questions," Hal Gregerson of MIT's *Questions Are the Answer*, and, of course, Great Books discussion groups, St.

John's College courses or Plato's *Dialogues* as examples of the question-based, Socratic method.

Unique Contributions

As we seek to earn influence in conversations, we can look for the **unique** opportunities around the edges and overlaps of what's valued and needed.

One way to find what's unique is to look at the first principles (simplest foundational ideas and assumptions) and root causes (early steps in a causal chain, assumptions, and underlying science or psychology) underlying each element of your shared goals. If you are talking about increasing impact, look at your marketing, messaging, and underlying customer personas, their needs and values. If you are talking about operational efficiency goals, consider people, processes and systems, inputs, work flows, and outputs. When you see overlaps in root causes or disconnects between first principles and current practice, then you may have identified a unique and relevant opportunity.

Another way to uncover potential unique contributions is to analyze the element of time in value creation. How might you speed up steps in the processes you share with other teams or even within your team? What might cut the time in half or double the throughput? While this might seem impossible at first, allow your mind to explore even wild ideas. You might hit on something that makes the "impossible" possible (a real-world example of this a bit later in this chapter).

Doing what others thought was impossible will earn you great visibility and influence with your team and beyond.

Becoming Visible

Being an introvert, my nature is to carefully manage my visibility. I don't want to be the oversharer on Facebook, the person touting their own accomplishments, or faking it until I make it.

I try to make things visible only as it serves a desire to legitimately earn influence based on a morally valuable end goal and a resonant, well-informed view of reality.

The decision of **when** to release information and become visible is critical. I prefer stealth mode, just quietly meeting one on one to ensure that things are moving on the right track, and then gradually increasing visibility as plans solidify and risks are reduced.

For me, one-on-one conversations are more connective and communicative than larger meetings, so I start sharing and becoming visible with individuals first. That way, I can quietly test and refine my ideas with trusted colleagues. Then, I set meetings with a few influential people in the organization to begin increasing my visibility organically. At the end of these one-on-one meetings with influencers, I like to offer a shareable artifact (a one pager, slide deck, memo or white paper) they can share with others.

Shareable artifacts are critical to improving your visibility. If possible, ensure influencers will benefit from sharing what you create by making it as relevant to them as possible. Include your personal contact information clearly but inconspicuously, on all shareable artifacts. This ensures that you become more visible as others carry your message to the world and that people can find you when they have questions or needs.

Another way to be visible is to be physically present. Work quietly and methodically to earn the influence required to be naturally, purposefully invited to the important meetings in your organization. The best way to be invited is to make yourself relevant, of course.

Also, try to attend the webinars, conferences and other industry events attended by the people just above your current level. Do your best to include yourself in the leadership of a business unit or organization whenever possible. As Stacy Abrams recently said,

> Never tell yourself no. Let someone else do that.

Additionally, if you have found your way into a large project, I suggest that you build project tracking into your collaboration platform (Asana, Slack, SharePoint, etc.). Create project update decks and / or make short update videos for the team that can also be shared to others across your organization. These can not only transfer information, but will also become lasting, visible evidence of how you think, work, and lead.

The key is to focus on first making it useful to those who might spread it for you. By aligning your purposes with their desire to be relevant, unique and visible, you will allow others to help you earn more influence as well. The fine line is to make sure it's not so obviously self-serving that no one wants to share it. Make it so your boss, friends, or other influencer can show off how great she or her team is, or so your team can show off the cool thing they're working on. For wider exposure, you might consider creating a project on your LinkedIn profile so your key team members can join that project and share that they are contributing to significant work.

With these ideas in hand, how do we organize our thinking and actions as we earn more influence? We built a wisdom jig so that you can internalize the method. See the jig on the next page.

Earned Influence = RUV Wisdom Jig

List of things I could do to earn influence that might be relevant and unique. Brainstorm and list possibilities here:

Relevance v. Uniqueness– sort things you could do into this matrix.

	Not Unique	Unique
Relevant	Might be a useful foundation for earning influence	**Earn influence with these**
Not Relevant	Avoid	Might be fun if time

Ways to be more visible doing the relevant, unique items. Places to be seen, critical gatherings and moments, shareable artifacts to create.

n.b Don't forget to schedule some time on your calendar to put your ideas into action. Try to work on earning more influence a little bit every day.

To Do	Due Date	On Calendar

You can download a pdf of this wisdom jig from our website.

Case Study: Opportunity Creation in a Large Firm

In 2010, I moved to southern Oregon without a job, so I had a chance to experiment with creating opportunities for myself. I felt like I knew how to make business operations and sales more effective and more profitable, so I applied for some jobs with a struggling company in town. It was a large, vertically integrated seasonal business with 1,500 full-time staff that swelled to nearly 6,000 in the holiday season.

I applied for some corporate director level and VP level jobs I knew I could handle, but I got no responses from the HR team. So, in October of 2010, I walked into their job center where they recruited the thousands of seasonal laborers they needed each year.

I walked up to the counter and said, "I know how to drive a forklift and I know how to use a computer, what do you have?" After a computer skills test, they said "Forget the forklift. We have some computer-heavy jobs for you. I see you have database and distribution experience. Would you like to interview for a job as an analyst in the distribution planning department?"

In the interview I learned that I would be analyzing operational data to troubleshoot shipments that missed their delivery dates. As a gift company, on-time delivery was critical to customer satisfaction and with four million packages of perishable product to deliver in six weeks, the holiday rush was going to be intense for whoever took this job.

Before I walked into their job center, I had already owned three different businesses, sold them and had been partially retired for several years. The job offered me less than eighteen dollars per hour, I had to punch a clock, and got almost no vacation, but I was happy to be inside the beast; I figured that if the company was healthy at all I would be able to work my way up into the core team that would turn the company around.

On my first day, they gave me a computer in the middle of an old packing house that had been converted into open office space by adding gray carpet and gray paint. To enter the space I had to stoop to walk down a dark hallway that was barely taller than I was. In the heart of the office space, a massive wooden beam was six inches lower than my height, so I had to duck under it many times per day. It was very much like working on floor 7 ½ in the film, *Being John Malkovich*. So, my surreal adventures in corporate America began.

Shocked and dismayed, I quietly sat down and started asking questions. "What can I do today that's relevant and unique?" I listened and I learned for weeks as my permissions for various databases and servers came online. Piece by piece, I began to assemble a mental map of our complex, vertically integrated 80 year old operations. The company owned the land, the trees and all the steps of production and distribution all the way to Grandma's house. If anything went wrong, I needed to understand what happened, how, and why.

As I thought about relevance, it's important to note that I was not thinking about my job title, but I was thinking about what the business and its clients needed. Because I had always been an owner, I always thought like one. Even without that experience, you can think as if you owned the place:

- What serves the organization and its customers?
- How would you want it to run?
- How could the firm be more efficient?

We discussed my efforts to identify and eliminate sources of costly errors in the last chapter, but my work soon exceeded my role. Instead of asking for permission, I simply took the relevant and unique steps of figuring out how we might reduce or eliminate those error sources no matter where they might be across the company. Soon, I was asking questions, solving problems and making myself visible in the IT, merchandising, and production departments as well as in the refrigerated warehouses.

About nine months after I started, my boss called me into his office and told me, "I really respect people who always work to make their own boss look good." I let his implied request hang in the air, then replied flatly that I could promise to do things correctly. I knew that my earned influence was increasing, but I was more committed to being relevant to the company and clients than to protecting him.

Over time, I found ways to become more visible. I started "bumping into" and talking directly to my boss' boss, the senior vice president of operations, about business questions I thought might be relevant to him. In meetings, I would try to ask relevant questions and make uniquely useful contributions, volunteering for every follow-up or collaboration possible in order to build stronger relationships across the company.

On the more complicated documents I created for my boss, I put in the footer in a faint gray type the simple statement, "Questions?" and added my email address.

This made it clear to anyone my boss shared the document with whose thinking was behind it and who could help with clarifications and related projects. I wanted something innocuous enough that even my boss wouldn't feel the need to remove it. I preplanned that if he questioned me about it, I would say, "If you get stuck in a meeting, or if someone is reading the presentation afterwards, and they wonder about the data and analysis, I want to make sure people can get answers without bothering you with details like that." Perhaps it was a bit passive aggressive, but dysfunctional organizations sometimes require some covert aggression in the service of the greater good for the organization and its stakeholders.

Within a year, the director above me resigned and I was promoted to his position. On his last day, he asked me not to make any immediate, drastic improvements to avoid embarrassing him. I told him I would try, but business requirements would drive changes.

Budgeting was underway for the coming year and I saw another opportunity to earn influence with something relevant and unique.

After studying the team's processes for sources of error and waste, I proposed some significant changes in the way the department was staffed for the peak season. In my studies, I came across Lean Six Sigma process redesign principles, and saw that eliminating spikes in workflow could improve efficiency.

That simple steady and calm smoothing of the workload let us hire only a few really good people. In the hiring process, we tested the candidates on the key skills of sorting quickly and paying attention to detail by using decks of playing cards and stopwatches.

These changes resulted in a reduction of both unit costs and error rates by forty percent. In just a couple of months the changes saved the firm a couple of hundred thousand dollars.

Suddenly, I was a very, very profitable employee for the SVP of operations, who started making me more visible by sending me to more interdepartmental coordination and project meetings. Based on these early successes, I was later given the opportunities to run the Voice of the Customer team, a Customer Experience and Satisfaction Data project.

Slowly at first, but accelerating over three years, I was able to move from making eighteen dollars an hour with no direct reporting employees to being the director of the business gift division, which had responsibility for a third of the firm's revenues and one hundred fifty employees in peak season. Granted, I started artificially low and not everyone will have the skills and opportunities I did, but very simply, this approach to earning influence worked.

Learning to Be Relevant

My rise at the retailer was based on my ability to learn relevant models and skills quickly.

Given the pace of opportunities opening up before us each day, leaders need to be "autodidacts," or self-teachers.

Because leaders need an ever broadening and deepening set of tools to use and then teach their teams, the only efficient way to gain knowledge is by pursuing exactly the knowledge you need, when you need it. Generic preset courses of study are unlikely to fit your specific focus and timing needs.

As we earn influence, generally the more tools you know how to use, the more relevant you are. In most workplaces, the most important tools are thinking tools. The unique differentiators to better thinking are:

Critical thinking skills– basic logic and logical fallacies

First principles and mental models from a variety of disciplines:

- **Physical**– physics, biology, chemistry, ecosystems, math through calculus (concepts, not a lot of problem sets), any basic sciences foundational or adjacent to your field of work.
- **Social**– psychology, sociology
- **Business**– organizational development, finance, micro, macro and behavioral economics, process modeling and re-engineering, any subjects adjacent to your current work.
- **Philosophical**– epistemology (how do we know things), authority and democracy, value systems
- **Historical**– great people and pivotal moments, start anywhere that is relevant to your own history or place

in the large cultural themes unfolding today– technology, equality, foundations of democracy

Subject matter expertise across your value chain

- The inputs to your value creation processes
- Your processes and similar processes in other fields
- Uses and impacts of the value you create

Rhetoric and Grammar– methods of clear expression and persuasion

Does this take time? Yes. Does every minute you invest contribute to your ability to be relevant and unique in every minute after that? Yes.

Reading this book is only the beginning of a long, beautiful, fruitful journey. Don't worry, Warren Buffet, Charlie Munger, Bill Gates, Elon Musk, and Ray Dalio have all made vast fortunes by thinking better than others using these exact methods. This is simply the smartest investment for most humans in most moments so we will return to the topic in chapter eleven. Being an autodidact is a key to earning your right to lead.

Pursuing Power for Good

Too many people pursue leadership positions and the power they offer for the wrong reasons: ego, control, fear. Humane leaders seek to earn influence so they can make relevant contributions in support of their shared core values.

Bertrand Russell wrote about power and its abuse in the late 1930s as fascists rose to power across the English Channel. He proposed that four conditions allowed a leader to pursue power with moral clarity:

- Power should be pursued as a means to some end so great that it dwarfs the goal of power itself.
- Power should serve the needs of others.
- The means to gaining power should not be inhumane or immoral to the point that the means do not justify the ends.
- The moral compass of the leader should orient to truth and honesty, not manipulation and propaganda.

While composed in a trying historical moment, these four conditions can still serve us as we pursue the power to lead.

- Are we leading our team toward better performance building upon moral clarity, or have we wandered off into less savory territory?
- How can you avoid temptation and get back on track?
- How might you strengthen your connection to your highest and best values as you pursue influence?

> The measure of a man is what he does with power.
>
> — Plato

Power, Pride and Unique Self Relevance

We often equate leaders and large egos. Some people who find large, needy egos repellent avoid leadership roles for fear of becoming like these tiny-hearted "big men." Unfortunately, there's a lot of evidence to support their concerns.

This mistaken conflation of aspects of our humanity creates two terrible outcomes:

- It keeps many thoughtful people from seeking leadership positions.
- The pushy and ego-driven find easy access to unclaimed leadership positions

The terrible shall inherit the Earth if the thoughtful and principled let them.

Pride and the ego that feeds on it are not by nature evil. It is natural and empowering to take pride in our own and our team's accomplishments. Ego becomes destructive when we let it cloud our moral clarity. Can we incorporate healthy ego and pride into our leadership?

Pride and ego are important foundations in legitimacy, referential, and expertise-based power. While many Eastern practices suggest that ego is the source of all suffering, it may also be our path forward. Humane leaders must dance with the challenging duality of ego.

Pride seems to be based in some sense of ownership of outcome. As we discussed in the last chapter, any sense of ownership of an uncontrollable outcome will be fraught with two perils of ego; winning by blind luck unnaturally inflates our egos and losing by bad luck artificially deflates our ego's natural functioning. But, what if we can be proud of who and how we are without being tied unrealistically to outcomes?

What if our state of being, our ontology, is our source of pride?

That you exist is amazing, that you show up, lead with moral clarity, fair strength, generative care, and wise balance is work to be proud of. Is it possible that all our manic **doing** feels so important because we've forgotten the power and wonder of our essential **being**?

This is not to say that we can simply be great without doing great things. But, is it possible that our work in the world will be far more powerful and meaningful if it comes from a foundation of ontological integrity and self-knowledge?

The key is that we can never fill gaps in our self worth with more accomplishment. The trouble starts when we compromise our values and settle for external measures of success– to get things done, gain a bit more recognition, or collect a little more money.

What is the cost of a short-sighted, teleological approach to self worth; the ends (my deliverables in this life) justify the means (my very existence)? While it is important to be a contributing member of society rather than a sponge, so many of us take being a contributing member of society too far. We keep pushing for more proof (our great work) of the unprovable (our worth).

Choosing New Sources of Self

Let's step back and ask, what parts of life's opportunities and responsibilities can we realistically control and hook our sense of self to?

Is it possible that we can be responsible for very little? With concerted effort and a lot of missteps, I only seem to be able to control who I am with others and how I do things. Given this realization, I now seek to simply:

- **Connect**– I can attempt to be present with the essential humanity of the people I engage with each day.
- **Clarify**– I can honestly seek to clarify the muddles we each find ourselves in. What might be true underneath all the confusion and chatter?
- **Create**– I can seek to deliver more value than I ask in return each day by doing things aligned with my values of service, quality and efficiency.

I can barely control these three inputs, much less outcomes that rely on huge webs of human and logistical dependencies. As leaders we should try our best to manage all the dependencies, but humane leaders draw a clear distinction between what's controllable and what's not. To do any less is a path to madness and disease.

For example, in my consulting work one day, I grew quite bored with a competitive analysis project for a global technology distributor. My motivation, engagement and productivity were low. I realized that I was not working in alignment with my own values and sense of service and quality.

So, I asked myself why I was doing the work and who would be served. I realized that I had no direct human connection in the project. The client was, to me, only a voice on the phone.

To engage and empower my desire to serve a real human, I pulled an image of the VP of Marketing who sponsored the analysis off of his LinkedIn profile and pasted it into the top of my working document. I imagined the tremendous pressure he felt from above and his attachment to his young family. Suddenly, my own pride was tied to serving this human who had succeeded in reaching a pinnacle of competing values, imperatives, and stress.

I knew that he was stressed enough to bring in expensive consultants like our firm to support his efforts. So, while I was ambivalent about the corporation, this man, this one human, I could proudly serve with everything I had. In the end, I delivered a competitive analysis that served the VP and supported my own search for meaning, personal pride, and connection.

By returning to what aligned with my values and what I could control, I was able to act with integrity and authenticity, which is one of the most unique and personally relevant contributions anyone can make.

You have a unique set of variables you can control today, this week. How will you use these opportunities?

Charting Time: Leader as Cartographer

Unstructured time is like a gray sea stretching before us. It's easy to get lost. Schedules created by others give us comfort, so most people work in very short jaunts organized by others, one day at a time. They may allow themselves to venture out into the sea a short distance (an hour meditating or a weekend retreat), but then hurry back to the familiar, predictable shore. Most of us only take on very small, discrete projects outside of our daily work. But others, like entrepreneurs, inventors, and artists, set out on long pilgrimages with uncertain destinations.

Leaders are cartographers of time who create their own maps to help us cross wild open spaces and vast oceans. These maps are visionary and mere suggestions based on little more than prior experience, insights, and intuitions.

Organizations, by nature, structure time to coordinate activities. Leaders, by definition, design, build, and maintain time structures to give their fellow travelers a sense of clarity, safety, and order.

Leaders break down the firm's multi-year strategic plans into annual plans, a team's quarterly milestones, weekly sprints and daily tasks assigned to individuals. But, they are also the ones who help team members build personal connections of purpose, meaning, and consciousness with the chart as well.

- Why does this map matter to me?
- How does it relate to who I aspire to be?
- How do I keep this in mind as my day wildly unfolds?

Leaders who fail to create and navigate with these time maps have teams that lack direction, cohesion, and effectively coordinated action plans. These failures lead to a lack of team engagement and progress. In the end these failures show up as turnover as well as declining productivity, revenue and profitability growth. Again, a failure of performance started as a failure of leadership.

Some leaders mistake activity for progress. They feel lulled into complacency when the team is busy. Really effective leaders will chart the course and set the pace of travel for the team and organization's work. Does the team move at a stately ("Let's meet on that next week") or frenetic ("Do that now") pace?

Some sleepy firms move at the pace of Samuel Barber's *Adagio for Strings* (38 beats per minute) while others try to move at the at the lively but exhausting pace of Bach's *Italian Concerto BWV 971 - Part 3 : Allegro Vivace* (172 beats per minute). Really experience these paces to gauge your own; treat yourself by listening to these pieces on a streaming service or YouTube. Each tempo has a role in our lives, but which is appropriate for your team today? s

Ideally, the leader sets a humane and inspiring variety of tempos in each week, something like Bach's *Toccata and Fugue in D minor BWV 565*. Think about how you might design and influence the pace of your team's work across time. Of course, Agile methods are one useful way teams blend a variety of tempos as they work.

Interruptions: Out of Control Tempo

In reality, organizations by nature, generate almost constant interruptions and distractions. Leaders must therefore work intelligently and creatively with interruptions.

Of course, we must learn to manage our time to maintain focus on deep analytical and creative work. But Peter Drucker pointed out that interruptions represent important opportunities for leaders to shape the culture, thought, and action of their team members. In some ways, a leader's job is to be interrupted by the realtime needs of the team for adjustment, correction, or encouragement.

Interruptions are your teammates coming to you with important signals about the realities they are facing internally and externally as they work. Each interruption reveals an opportunity to shape values and priorities while also learning about the needs of your team for encouragement, empowerment, or development. In each of those moments of the culture of the organization and the capability of your team are shaped and improved if you are responding in an edifying way.

If you're getting repeated interruptions from the same person who could have decided something for himself, that's important data too; there's a need to develop your processes, your team or both. If a leader shuts herself off from interruptions and the data they contain, she's shutting herself off from the realities of her organization. So, leaders must allow time for interruptions each day by designing public access to their daily calendars, much like a professor's office hours are set in advance.

What's Relevant Now

Leaders must hold what's most relevant across the jumbled expanse of time. The well-known Eisenhower matrix helps sort the relevant from the unimportant. Effective leaders work on what is important but not urgent, while most people default to working on what is urgent but less strategically important.

As a refresher, here's an Eisenhower matrix:

Not Urgent	Time wasters	**Humane leaders work strategically here**
Urgent	Many people work here	Crisis leaders and reactive doers work here
	Not Important	Important

Of course, sometimes leaders must step down into the urgent to support the team's work. But, leaders, by definition, lead the organization towards significant strategic progress.

To use time effectively on important but not urgent, strategic work requires careful planning and project analysis, topics covered in our next chapter. For now, let's assume the leader has a good, clear plan. This plan will make clear what is relevant now; what should be done when, and by whom.

The leader's job is to structure the team's work in time. While it can be easy to know what to do next, it's much harder to hold what's relevant at each step across weeks and months. Unfortunately, no one but the leader is empowered to hold this role. Even with a project manager, the leader plays a critical role in protecting the team from one of the most fearsome forces in the universe, entropy.

Entropy of Consciousness: Holding Focus Across Time

Our best laid plans are subject to a dark force; entropy of consciousness. I bet you can find half a dozen forgotten visions and beautifully crafted plans in your files.

Entropy n.

1. *Physics– A thermodynamic quantity representing the unavailability of a system's thermal energy for conversion into mechanical work, often interpreted as the degree of disorder or randomness in the system.*
2. *Lack of order or predictability; gradual decline into disorder.*

The idea of entropy can also be applied to order and chaos in a system like our team and its projects. Creating plans and building processes, systems and organizations requires huge amounts of psychic, physical and mechanical energy. In many ways, order in our consciousness is the same. It takes effort to develop and maintain good habits of mind and body, to create and act consistently with our own plans.

As in the material world, our own consciousness is subject to entropy. Do you remember what you planned last night to do this morning or were you distracted by something more urgent or shiny?

What about your detailed plan for the quarter? Is that still top of mind for you? If so, how did you add energy to your system to keep it there? What about your five year plan?

If leaders struggle with entropy of consciousness, imagine how your team suffers. Are you offering them structures to re-energize their consciousness about the plan, the roadmap, and your agreed processes?

The structure I use is a nested series of daily, weekly, and monthly meetings to regularly recharge the order of my plans in my mind; to "re-mind" myself and my team. Each meeting is organized around a series of questions:

- What are we doing and why?
- Is our plan working?
- What changes shall we experiment with given what we've learned so far?

These questions shape and re-energize our consciousness.

Questions, by means of the Socratic method, form the roots of Western civilization and are still hugely powerful. If I ask you, "What did you have for breakfast today?" I just radically reshaped your consciousness around a topic I chose. When I ask, "Why did you have that?" I extend your consciousness into the revealing realms of your culture, habits, and motivations. Humane leaders use questions to shape and focus consciousness.

As leaders, we can use questions and a thoughtful cadence of meetings to shape and focus our own and our team's consciousness around our plans and how they relate to time. If you don't, who else will keep the team focused on next steps, priorities, and timing?

Leaders Start and Restart

After a team's collective deliberation and formation of a plan, the leader says, "Yes, let's go!" and jumps toward the first step. Others naturally join this courageous, clear energy. As social animals we all love to be led towards adventures we've had a hand in choosing.

After an exciting start, the team will inevitably return to disorder over time as entropy of consciousness takes hold. Then, the leader will need to restart the team and project by adding clarity and energy to the system.

> **Begin**– to begin is half the work, let half still remain; **again begin** this, and thou wilt have finished.
>
> — Aurelius, *Meditations*

Holding the team's consciousness of what's relevant (the plan) across time, starting and restarting the second, third, and hundredth time, the leader maintains the consistent fetch (more on this in chapter ten) that gets big important projects done.

Time to Invest In Your Own Power

Leaders make investment decisions with every dollar allocated to labor, equipment, and materials, and especially with every minute of their day. Our most precious investment, time, is also the key to our making our unique contributions.

> To fill the hour– that is happiness; to fill the hour and leave no crevice for a repentance.
>
> This day's travel, a journey, is made up of hours. This moment is **our time to do our work.**
>
> To finish the moment, to find the journey's end in every step of the road, to live the greatest number of good hours, is wisdom.
>
> — Emerson, *Journals*

But, what if we invested our hours in multiplying our own ability to lead and contribute? What if we turned our own unique gifts (genius), power, time, and money towards investing in our ability to make more of an impact?

> As long as your genius buys, the investment is safe, though you spend like a monarch. [Each person has a unique gift and this] guides his labor and his spending.
>
> The merchant's economy is a coarse symbol of the soul's economy. It is, to spend for power, and not for pleasure.
>
> The true thrift is always to spend on the higher plane; to invest and invest, with keener avarice, that he may spend in spiritual creation, and not in augmenting animal existence.
>
> — Emerson, "Wealth"

Your unique gift

> Nature arms each man with some faculty which enables him to do easily some feat impossible to any other, and thus makes him necessary to society.
>
> — Emerson, "Wealth"

- What is that contribution you can so easily make?
- Are you investing heavily in your one, unique gift?
- If not, why not?
- Look into the root causes of your underinvestment in your own gifts.

These words you are reading are the result of me asking myself these same questions. Lead yourself humanely, take a moment to ponder these questions.

Our most important work is the creative application of our unique skills and experiences– whether in accountancy, building, surgery, or portraiture. Of course, the most precious investment we can make in our own art forms is our own time. Unfortunately, we are often the worst interrupters of our own most creative, meaningful, fulfilling efforts.

Mary Oliver, in her essay "Of Power and Time," calls for each of us to honor our unique creative impulses with the hours and energy required for their fruitfulness. Don't give your own artistry, contributions, and fulfillment short shrift.

Are you an artist? Is your work creative?

If you think not, I invite you to think again. First, consider that an artist is someone who works to express something, to capture something, to create a felt difference in another human being. Do you seek to make a felt difference in another human through our daily efforts? Do you still hope for that? Reframing our work as art (Latin, **ars,** for skill, craft or power) re-energizes our original, most hopeful visions for our life's work.

Investment of time and money in equipping your highest faculties is not selfish if your intention is to serve others and higher values– see again Bertrand Russel's four conditions of pursuing power for good.

Remember that we are at all moments a living example to everyone we touch. So, any investment in your own power for high purposes will make you a powerful example of a life well lived.

Further reading

- Aurelius, *Meditations*, 2nd century
- Drucker, *The Effective Executive*, 1966
- Emerson, "Wealth," an essay in *The Conduct of Life*, 1860
- Emerson, *Journals*, finally published in 1982
- Gregersen, *Questions are the Answer*, 2018
- Hagstrom, *Latticework*, 2000– Warren Buffet's and Charlie Monger's development of their own thinking skills
- Parrish, Farnam Street blog at fs.blog– search on "Mental Models"

- Plato, *Dialogues,* Start with Meno, fourth century BCE
- Oliver, "Of Power and Time" in *Upstream: Selected Essays*, 2016
- Russell, Power: *A New Social Analysis,* 1938
- Tippet & Whyte, *On Being Project,* "The Conversational Nature of Reality"

10

Excellent performance requires clarity of expectations.

Of the variables in the MOCA model of performance, clarity of expectations is the easiest and most empowering variable for leaders to control.

Making expectations clear to your team is like putting your hands on the handlebars and your feet on the pedals of a bicycle. It puts you back in the seat of control over both the direction and pace of your team in order to reach your destination expeditiously.

There's one transformative assumption every leader should make:

If I am the leader, then I assume every problem is a leadership problem.

Leaders disempower themselves when they look at poor performance and think, "They…"

The self empowering position is, "What can I do to lead this person towards higher performance?"

Here are a few very basic examples

They	I, the leader, will
Forgot to do it	Create clear project management processes and habits as well as checklists for routine tasks
Didn't balance competing priorities	Review and energize team focus and priorities in daily standup meetings and regular project updates
Didn't get what they needed from person X	Identify and orchestrate all handoffs and dependencies across teams and silos
Didn't know you wanted it done that way	Create and acculturate processes for all important functions in your value chain

Leadership = Delegation

The process of clearly communicating expectations to another human is at the heart of delegation. Delegation:

- **Extends** your own thoughts into action by others.
- **Engages** and grows others you delegate work to.

- **Allows** others to contribute to team goals.

Most delegation failures stem from four common mistakes.

- **Uninspiring plans** creating structural low performance.
- **Inaccurate or incomplete plans** that are missing steps, order of operations, and dependencies between tasks.
- **Lack of precise, deliverable expectations** clearly communicated.
- **Ignoring entropy of consciousness** and its antidote, fetch.

By planning and leading projects well, you can create great clarity of expectations to help improve your team's performance.

Beautiful Plans

Leaders help the team envision and plan clear, inspiring work.

A humane leader engages their team's experience, knowledge, and creativity to build a clear, precise plan that balances efficient, effective actions with the flexibility to adapt to new data. Leaders understand that a plan is simply a written record of the team's best data and thinking at the moment. The relevance, elegance and actionability of the plan define its value and beauty.

Beautiful plans do more than clearly structure work, they can also be wellsprings of inspiration. For a plan to reach the level of beautiful inspiration, it must be audacious enough to be worth pursuing with everything we've got. Only the leader can help a team call itself to this level of vision and courage.

The person who calls the team to courageous vision and action often becomes the de facto leader. The students of Parkland High School, Malala Yousafzai, and Greta Thunberg usurped the leadership roles of the most powerful men on Earth by the moral clarity and audacity of their vision and expression.

One way to create relevant and audacious goals is to ask three questions I created after reading an article on the global industrial firm ABB's efforts to cut their cycle times.

I call these questions Double, Half, Half:

- How can we double our impact, throughput or sales?
- How can we cut costs in half?
- How can we cut cycle time in half?

Leaders must ask bigger, more important questions than anyone else on the team because this helps redefine what's possible. For instance, Curt Carslon of the Stanford Research Institute led teams that took on and solved important problems like voice control for mobile devices (Siri) and HDTV.

After many years leading SRI, Curt is now teaching the practice of innovation to other leaders and their teams. In an interview with Todd Miller for SFGate, Curt said,

> If you stick to the fundamentals of great people, great values, every one aligned, it's not like work.... It feels like having a good time with my buddies.

> I'm doing things that matter and it'll make a positive contribution.

Leaders are the ones who create the team, values, and alignment. When we asked Curt about that experience of transcendent collaboration, he described working as a professional violinist in an ensemble. The group had an experience of absolute bliss after performing a piece together. The players looked at each other dumbstruck, thinking, "My god, that was amazing. Look what we just did together, this almost spiritual experience of collaboration and creation." He sought to recreate that experience every day with his teams at SRI.

Creating audacious, visionary plans as a team is a productive and humane path forward because it creates the sense of purpose, connection, and meaning we all seek.

> Make no little plans. They have no magic to stir men's blood and probably themselves will not be realized.
>
> Make big plans; aim high in hope and work, remembering that a noble, logical diagram once recorded will never die, but long after we are gone will be a living thing, asserting itself with ever-growing insistency. Remember that our sons and grandsons are going to do things that would stagger us.
>
> Let your watchword be order and your beacon beauty.
>
> Think big.
>
> — Daniel Burnham

Inspiring Creative Reach

Elegant balance of inspiration and sustained clarity is the key to successful plans and their execution.

> All men dream: but not equally.
>
> Those who dream by night in the dusty recesses of their minds wake in the day to find that it was vanity: but the dreamers of the day are dangerous men, for they may act their dreams with open eyes, to make it possible.
>
> This I did.
>
> — T. E. Lawrence

Creative courage, skills, methods, and resources are required to reach way up into the ethers of creative inspiration to grab a visionary idea to bring to reality on Earth.

Consider this illustration of the creative process.

Level of Creativity	Requires
Ideal Impossible Invisible / Unseen	Vision
Improbable Mirage-like Improved	Courage and persuasion
In process Building	Skill and resources
Real Done Visible	Focused effort and learning across time

Urgency usually lives down in the real world, while visionary, transformative leadership reaches far up into the ideal, not-yet real which is important, but not yet urgent. Leaders hold the tension between the ideal and optional versus the real and urgent demands of the organization. It is not enough to overly focus on one or the other, the leader must hold both in order to make what's possible real.

Engage your team in breaking down an audacious vision into a set of discrete, action-oriented, increasingly challenging milestones to work towards. Adjust your goals often (at least monthly) based on what you've experimented with and learned along the way.

Clarity: Project Leadership

Creating and holding clarity over time is the leader's greatest opportunity to make a positive impact by bringing courageous visions into reality. Project management is the art and science of creating and holding this clarity on complex projects like building skyscrapers or launching rockets. Project leadership takes project management and makes it a tool for team inspiration, motivation and development over time.

While professional project managers spend years perfecting their craft, successful project leaders only need a firm grasp of project management first principles which include:

- Project definition and launch processes.
- Critical path identification.
- Resource and time allocation using Gantt charts.
- Identifying and relieving risks and constraints.

Learning these first principles and how to use them will bring clarity and discipline to your work. If you are lucky enough to have a project management team in your organization, knowing these principles will improve your collaboration with them.

Project leadership is work for the entire team. The leader must do their best to define and communicate the plan clearly, but then clarity becomes a shared responsibility. Clarifying the path forward becomes a fast paced dance between the team and the leader to sharpen focus, define edges, reduce risks, and orchestrate timings. The team must clarify their own roles and contributions early and fast, using all of their experience and best thinking to preemptively identify and head off potential problems as they appear, but before they arrive.

Leaders must be aware that passive aggressive team mates may refrain from mentioning any lack of clarity until it's too late, damaging the team's morale or delaying the project. See the section on passive aggressive teammates in chapter six for specific approaches to turning this challenge to your advantage.

Elegance

Once our plans are big enough to stir our blood and clear enough to be made possible, we can then seek to make them elegant.

Elegance, to me, means pared down to essential clarity and simplicity. An interesting example of a truly elegant planner and designer is Dutch landscape architect Piet Oudolf who designed the plantings for the Highline in New York City and many gardens across Europe. Oudolf elegantly addresses the essential truths of plants and time by designing across all four seasons, choosing plants that are beautiful even after their flowers fade and others that are lovely covered in snow. He describes his own planting designs as a "layering of seasonality, energy, endurance and reward – both before, during and after flowering." (Pearson) Oudolf works with the simple truths of each plant's annual cycles to create an ingeniously harmonious and elegant experience in each season.

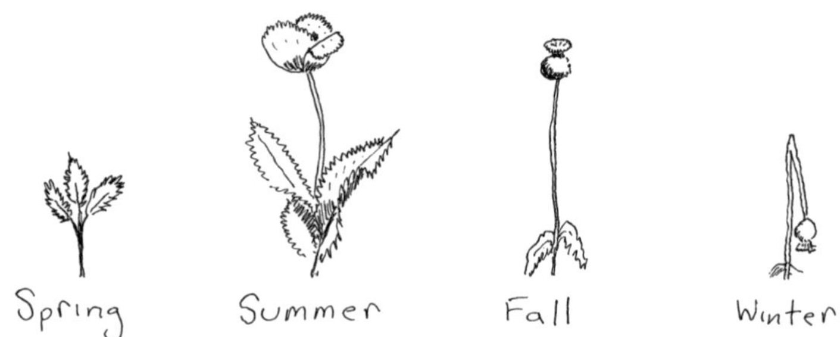

To bring elegance to your plans, you will need to understand the essential qualities of all the elements involved; people, processes and systems as well as the environment, inputs and outputs expected.

How can you and your team layer the complicated reality of your work and resources with your limited but expansive humanity and goals into an elegant, living plan?

Leaders, Thinking and Reality

It's fun to be a visionary leader, but making grand visions a reality requires foresight, skills, and courage.

Visionary leaders must get real quickly, clearly and often, understanding the value creation formula (variables and relationships) and hosting the collaborations required to refine the visions and realities of the path towards its completion.

Getting real quickly and clearly requires a leader to think excellently. Clear critical and synthetic thinking calls for:

- A precise definition and organization of the problem space.
- Complete, validated data.
- Categorization and analysis of data.
- A nuanced understanding of relationships between variables–correlation, causation, arithmetic, exponential, and any algorithmic relationships.
- Understanding dependencies and order of operations.
- Synthesis of findings into actionable insights.
- Hypotheses to test with further experiments.
- Evaluation of competing experiments based on valuation and prioritization schema.

Each step builds upon the prior steps, so early decisions are critical to correctly map to reality. That may be why McKinsey puts such energy into using MECE (sounds like Greece according to its creator, but many people say, me-see) to clarify and organize data. MECE stands for Mutually Exclusive, Comprehensively Exhaustive, a fancy way of asking, "Am I looking at the complete data set and can I clearly sort out the subsets within it?" McKinsey's approach is based on some well-tested thinking by Aristotle in his essay, Categories. A mistake in categorizing data will distort all the analysis that follows so take time to get this right. Early errors cost more than late ones because they are foundational for all that follows (Kuprenas and Frederick).

The quality of your thinking matters. To refine your thinking

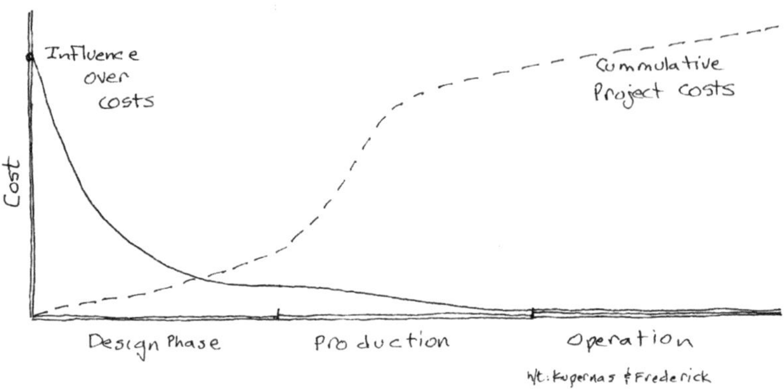

Early design thinking strongly influences total project costs

skills, add some of the classics of the genre to your reading list. Your skills will be refined by just doing the intellectual work required to follow their exquisite thinking. The purest forms of thinking are philosophy and mathematics. The easy place to start is with the Greeks, Plato's *Dialogues* and Euclid's *Elements.* More practically, start with Aristotle's *Categories* and continue on to Kreeft's *Socratic Logic* and learning the basic logical fallacies. Of course, read Descartes listed in the Further Reading section.

Armed with the basics, move into more recent, practical applications of clear thinking found in the theory of constraints (Goldratt), lean methodologies (George) and project management basics.

Tool: Dependency Trees

The thinking processes captured in the dependency tree method will improve your categorization, constraint and dependency analysis skills as well as the prioritization of competing urgencies. We'll explain the process and demonstrate it by mapping the elements required for a clear dependency tree by showing snippets of a dependency tree below.

Use the Dependency Tree Wisdom Jig when starting a new project to figure out:

- Where to start
- What needs to be done in what order
- Where to invest first to eliminate risks quickly
- How to ensure you meet your target dates

See the Wisdom Jigs page on the Humane Leadership website for a dependency tree template.

A quick overview of important methods before we begin the dependency tree process:

MECE

- Start with **comprehensively exhaustive**– try to clearly define the complete set of what you want in your desired end state.
- Then, work to break the end state into **mutually exclusive sub categories**. Define each subcategory in writing and look for the edge case examples to help you clearly draw lines of differentiation between the categories.

This is the foundational work that reduces costs later, so take your time.

Dependencies

- What does your goal or element of your goal depend upon? Every step of your project will depend upon some prior work, for instance, selling depends upon having a product, a pricing scheme, the ability to deliver, a sales team, and prospective client. More examples below.

Evaluation

- What do you value most in this project? Time, money spent, potential gains or avoiding risks?
- What values constrain your activities in this project? Financial, social, reputational, moral, or ethical concerns?
- Being clear about your values and constraints will help you decide on your approach and the prioritization of your efforts.

Prioritization

- Analyze the complete project to identify the critical path and the riskiest assumptions you want to prove. McKinsey calls this process derisking.
- Prioritize working on those steps that will eliminate the risks in assumptions and in the time required to complete your critical path.

Process for creating a dependency tree:

1. Start by clearly defining your goal. This can be done in a separate project plan document.
2. Turn your goal into a MECE sentence succinctly describing your goal or desired end state in the box at left on the wisdom jig.

We will double our
impact on local clients
and reduce our cost
to serve by 50%

3. Take keywords from your sentence and draw a line and write the words and make a box around it.
4. Add what would be required to create that outcome for each element, again, in boxes to the right connected with lines. Do this for each of your original three boxes (Local clients, Double our impact, etc.).
5. For each of the branches you just created, make

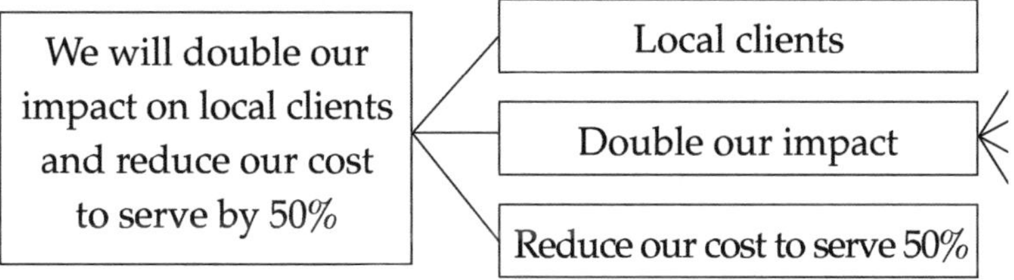

branches off of those until you have a granular tree of all the tasks your goal is dependent upon.

For example:

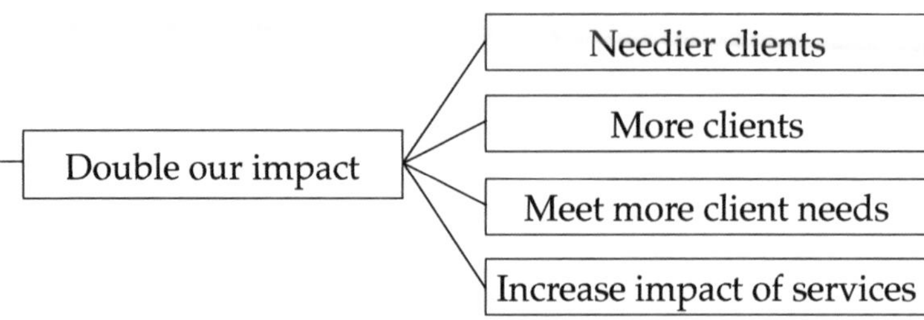

This process continues branching, usually 4-5 layers deep, until you get to clear, doable actions or decisions at the right edge of your page.

Extract Value from Your Dependency Tree

Now, begin to synthesize your analytical work into a usable project plan.

The items at the right edge should be pretty easily converted into actionable or delegatable tasks, with owners, due dates, and clearly defined, measurable deliverables. But, before we get to handing out assignments, we need to look at the project more closely.

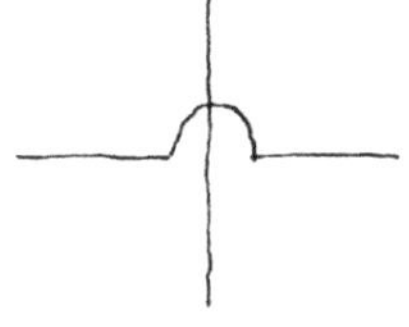

First, look for connections between elements across various branches. Draw lines between dependent items from different branches of the tree. These might reveal dependencies and risks that become really important later. To avoid getting messy, when two lines cross, you can make one line bump up over the other like electrical engineers do.

Next, double check your work by thinking backwards. Start at the right edge and ask if we did this step would we necessarily, almost automatically, meet our goal in the next higher step (to the left)? Is anything missing that's required to make the step to the left happen? If yes, add that to your tree in the appropriate place.

Once your dependency tree feels complete, circle the 3-5 elements most critical and or risky in reaching your goal. In our example, finding sources of local clients would certainly be on the list. If that doesn't happen early on, nothing else is worth doing.

Look at all of your tasks. Some tasks can run in parallel, but others must be done in order, for instance, onboarding new clients cannot be done until new client sources are identified. Which of your tasks can be done in parallel with each other and which must be done sequentially? Bold or highlight the lines connecting tasks that must be done sequentially.

Estimate the time required to do each task. Add up all the sequential times to your goal to see which path will take longest.

The longest path through these sequential items is your critical path; the path that you must follow as quickly as possible to your goal. Highlight the lines connecting those items on the critical path to make it quite obvious.

This is only a very basic critical path analysis. There is far more to it than we can cover in this book. Any investment you make in learning project management will be rewarded with greater clarity and effectiveness in all your future endeavors.

Gantt Charts

With your critical path in mind, create a list of important tasks and explain how we would clearly, measurably know that step is complete. Assign an owner to each task – they may not do all of the work themselves, but they will clearly own that the work gets done as planned.

For longer projects, build a Gantt chart to help you plan how these tasks will unfold over time.

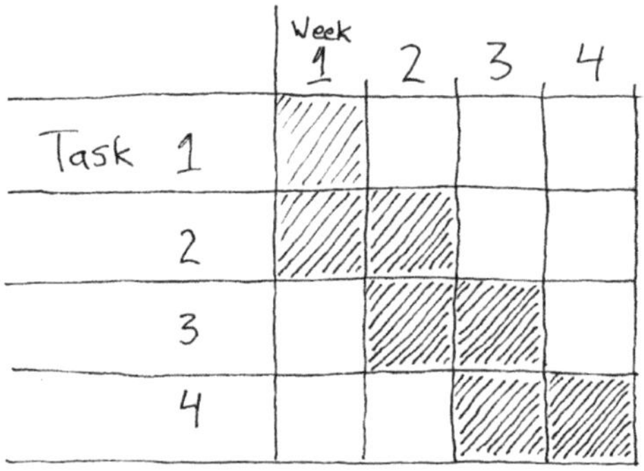

Gantt charts are very useful for planning the timeline, seeing if you have resource constraints (one person or tool that is overloaded in a certain time period) and for communicating status and next steps to the team and stakeholders quickly and clearly. Start moving your tasks from the dependency tree to your Gantt chart so that you can put them in order and decide when to start and end each step in your project.

When working with task timing and Gantt charts, ask three questions for every task:

- How soon can we start eliminating risks associated with this task?
- How could we cut the time derisking takes in half?

- Can we start experimenting right away?

These questions help us accelerate the derisking and eventual completion of the project.

To help you get started, a Gantt chart template is available on the Wisdom Jigs page on Humane Leadership website.

Meet to Manage the Critical Path

Finally, use project update meetings to support your team's performance. When should the team take a fresh look at all of this to see if things have changed? Next week, next month? Meetings, like checklists, are moments to focus the team's consciousness with important questions.

Plan the cadence of your meetings carefully and adjust to minimize time in meetings while maximizing clarity, alignment, motivation and progress toward your goal.

In each meeting, quickly cycle through these questions to reach your goal as soon as possible:

- Are we on track to meet our plan?
- Does our plan need to change?
- Are the tasks prioritized accurately?
- How can we lower the remaining risk in our plan?
- How can we accelerate and build momentum along the critical path?
- Which parallel tasks can be started now ?
- Are our resources being used effectively and efficiently?

- Can we see any constraints or bottlenecks ahead?

Set these follow up meetings on your calendar as soon as you have a plan. Set your meetings frequently at the beginning and in the few weeks leading up to the close of your project. Adjust your project meetings to build the team's momentum toward the goal. Some teams may need daily standup meetings while others may need only weekly reviews. Most teams cannot go two weeks without having their plan and priorities refocused and re-energized.

While we have focused on the traditional project management approach to ordering tasks into a critical path, you may find that other approaches yield important insights to your planning process. We suggest looking at Goldratt's The Goal which presents his theory of constraints. If you are working toward a product or application, consider using Agile and Lean Startup methodologies to organize your work. Find many good primers, courses and books online.

Methodical Planning and Humane Leadership

Project management is a very monochronic (linear time model in which one thing happens at a time), deductive and methodical approach to work. How can we reconcile this mechanism with humane leadership values?

We believe that clearly defined plans are useful expressions of all three humane leadership values:

- They show strength of character and mind and democratize the flow of information and the definition of work.

- They are generatively caring because they create opportunity for others to learn, grow, and contribute in new ways.
- They are wisely balanced because they minimize chaos and maximize the impact of the team's collective wisdom and effort.

Without clear plans, the humans in organizations will feel lost – not a recipe for engagement, empowerment and high performance.

At the same time, a well-planned project will soon lead the team to an alchemical moment that builds focus and momentum quickly. The really skilled humane leader will design these gusts of wind into their project plan and give their team a huge completed dopamine loop to engage them in pushing the project towards the huge impact you all hope for.

Entropy of Consciousness

Starting out strong on a good path is half of success, but the key to final delivery is staying on that path over time.

The great, forgotten plan is the bane of every leader's existence. Why?

Plans exist in our minds, and our minds are subject to the entropy of consciousness we discussed in the last chapter. So, how can we fight the entropy that lets us forget our elegant plans so easily?

Negentropy is the effort required to build and maintain order in a universe that seems set on destroying order and momentum. To leaders, negentropy requires that we communicate plans clearly and frequently to reenergize the team's consciousness on milestones, processes, and next steps.

Do not underestimate the energy required to hold your team's focus as their consciousness floats through time. This is why your cadence of update meetings is so important. To wit,

> ...there should be long OBEDIENCE in the same direction;
>
> there thereby results... something which has made life worth living; for instance, virtue, art, music, dancing, reason, spirituality– anything whatever that is transfiguring, refined, foolish, or divine.
>
> — Nietzsche

Who on your team gently and firmly holds this long obedience in the same direction? I believe that no one but the leader can hold long obedience. Who else will hold it if you do not?

Fetch: Fighting Entropy

But how, with all the distractions of modern life, can we possibly hope to fight the forces of entropy in our consciousness?

The meteorological concept of fetch may help. If we think of the ocean, we can imagine the water sits in calm chaos on a peaceful day, each molecule of H2O vibrating randomly. Our team is like this when left to its own devices for too long.

But, sometimes all of that water gets moving and crashes powerfully ashore.

The organization of the water into tall waves crashing ashore is determined by how strongly and how long the wind has been blowing across the water's surface. Because energy takes time to transfer from air to water, it takes time to organize water into big waves. A brief gust of wind will ripple the water but a few days of hurricane force winds howling across the surface of the ocean can build towering 100-foot waves.

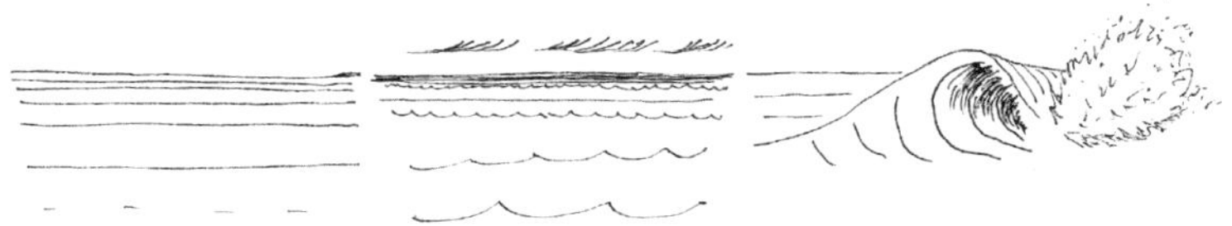

Your organization is like the ocean; it's full of chaotic, inert particles that can, with effort across time, be organized and energized to create the value and impacts you've envisioned.

Are you giving your best visions enough fetch to build towards their potentially monumental impacts on the shore?

Socratic Leadership: Fetching Questions

A leader's purposeful questions create a strong, consistent wind that creates fetch; I call this approach Socratic leadership.

Each question shapes consciousness and prompts action that improves performance. What set of questions would lead your team to better performance?

Go back and look at your dependency tree and its critical path to identify all the steps required to reach your goal.

Write questions you could ask yourself and others to:

- Accelerate critical path tasks.
- Build momentum along the critical path.
- Derisk the critical path.
- Think about double, half, half opportunities to increase your project's impact and your team's earned influence.

Ask yourself and key members of your team these questions regularly to find new paths toward our goal. Then, validate, refine and implement the best ideas collaboratively with your team.

Checklists: Persistent Questions

Of course, you cannot walk around asking questions all day. So how can you ask project and process structuring questions consistently across all the members of our team at once?

A well-designed process checklist is simply a structured series of questions that persists across time to shape consciousness, thought, and action.

> [Checklists] are quick and simple tools [that] by remaining swift and usable and resolutely modest, are saving thousands upon thousands of lives.
>
> — Gawande

You may not be doing surgery, but your work also deserves to be done consistently and efficiently. Other structured, persistent ways to pose questions include project plans, Gantt charts and regular progress review meetings, but checklists have the advantage of being asynchronous and customizable by role.

So, leader, use checklists based on the tasks captured in your dependency tree or work processes to structure your team's daily work. This creates a natural, repeatable input of the energy required to fight entropy of consciousness without you having to be present at every moment.

To be really effective at creating clarity of expectations across your team, each role should have its own daily, weekly and/or monthly checklists. For critical, highly detailed roles, like a surgeon, you may need a checklist per step in the process.

In most roles, a weekly checklist with a combination of daily tasks requiring attention, a set of tasks that need attention once per week and a space for any notes, questions, exceptions or learnings during the week works well. It is possible to also track hours on this same sheet for payroll or simple accountability purposes. Once you have the hours worked, this same sheet can track a few KPIs on a daily basis, such as sales calls per hour each day, etc. Adding a signature line creates more personal accountability for the person who turns in the checklist at the end of their work week.

Checklists create a set of clear tracks leading each person on a team towards their successful contribution. Of course, we know the train of our consciousness will derail, so the checklist allows us to quietly, quickly put the train back on the tracks. This is a recipe for employee engagement and excellent performance, even fulfillment for all involved.

> Happiness comes from expressing what we have rationally decided is good for us over the long term.
>
> — Aristotle

A nested series of checklists builds a structure that pushes the plan, updates and any exceptions to you each day. At the end of the day, each team member's checklist feeds into the team leader's checklist. That way, when the team lead shares their checklist with you, she is reporting on her own consciousness of the entire team's performance.

I prefer printed copies of checklists as they feel more real and less forgettable to me than digital copies. But, you can experiment to see what works best for yourself and your team. Being present to see a physical checklist allows for informal check ins at the end of the day. If you cannot be present, have your team members (or lead) take photos with their phones and upload them to a daily reporting folder. This is a simple way to create a digital version of the hard copy with a distributed team. Data can easily be pulled from the digital copies and added to KPI tracking data by a coordinator-level team member. This checklist data will also become raw material for analysis of performance at personal and team at performance review time.

The key to success is for leaders at all levels to ask follow up questions about what people are reporting on their checklists. Dig into the issues your team raises or the issues you see in the work they are reporting to you. Your team's questions and anomalies in data must prompt more questions (energy and clarity) from you, the leader. Without follow up questions each day, the checklists will soon become meaningless administrative overhead. Make these checklists the center of your team communications each day and you will see fetch building.

This is a very powerful technique that allowed me to leave my 35 employees for a month at a time before email was used in business. My team used nested checklists that rolled up into a one page operations manager checklist. This list was faxed once per week to hotels I stayed in as I travelled.

I would take that fax into a phone booth (pre cell phones, too) and ask detailed questions designed to shape the thinking and actions of various members of the team. "Ask salesperson X what their plan is to increase their calls per day and ask logistics supervisor Y what she's doing to increase stops per hour on route 3." Over time the checklists and this technique

Question and data flow on nested checklists

refined to the point where I could come home after a month away to no surprises, no backlog of work, and positive sales growth.

Of course, these checklists structure the work of the team, but they also allow the front line to share challenges, exceptions, learnings and questions with senior leadership in a feedback section at the bottom of each page.

Expectations From Below: Prodelegation

As leaders who serve the performance of our team, we are open to their requests for anything that might contribute to their success.

Prodelegation happens when workers delegate work up to leadership with the goal of more efficiently and effectively creating value. The word is a compound of:

- Pro– before or in front of.
- Delegation– to appoint or entrust duties to another.

It is critical to listen carefully to the prodelegation signals you receive from your team about their concerns, ideas, needs, and even excuses. The team may feel like they are tattling or complaining, but to a good leader this data is gold. I love hearing excuses, because when I eliminate the root cause of the complaint I have just eliminated one more reason my team might miss a milestone or KPI.

Humane performance improvement is not about coddling people, it's about being clear about what's needed from the person for the organization to reach new levels of performance.

Please note that prodelegation is not **reverse delegation**; that's when a person fails to perform and returns a delegated task to the leader for completion. Reverse delegation is a bad sign and should prompt the immediate scheduling of a MOCA performance improvement meeting.

Prodelegation empowers workers to be clear in their requests for help. This is a big responsibility because prodelegation is not simply pointing out what is wrong, it is proposing solutions the leader might be able to implement on behalf of the team.

The power of prodelegation is in defining the scope of a leader's responsibility. Front line workers in progressive organizations are increasingly demanding that their leaders take responsibility for the societal, environmental and ethical impacts of their decisions. Look at Google employee's demonstrations about senior leadership's dubious choices regarding sexual misconduct claims, the use of artificial intelligence in defense work, and censored search for China. These workers are prodelegating expanded social and environmental responsibility and improved decision making processes to senior leaders.

Defining Scope of Responsibility

Many of our greatest challenges stem from allowing leaders to define the scope of their own responsibilities.

If absolute power corrupts, part of that corruption sneaks in when leaders self-servingly decide to limit what they must consider when they make decisions and take action.

From this day forward we as leaders must be aware that we will likely experience prodelegation or defections if we conveniently ignore the health of our team members, our community, and the environment in pursuit of all-hallowed shareholder value. We've come a long way over the past 100 years with worker and consumer safety, but we still have many opportunities to more accurately link a leader's responsibilities to the impacts of their decisions.

We can also turn this entire performance improvement function around and use it to ask leaders to perform better, to become clearer about their own motivations, to use their time and authority more wisely, to clarify and communicate their realistic expectations more effectively, and to develop their leadership skills so that they can better support our success. 360 reviews are a good start, but imagine a day when team members support their leaders by holding their own performance improvement meetings with them. Courageous leaders will proactively ask their teams to use the P(MOCA) framework to help design leadership performance improvements and expanded responsibilities for themselves.

Morality is a responsibility we must demand of all leaders. The humane leadership values explained in chapter one are a simple place to start.

If you have the opportunity to lead, you have the responsibility to lead with competence and moral clarity based on shared values. Don't mistakenly believe that you have opportunity without accountability. Do the best you can with the opportunity you've been given because someone else didn't get that opportunity. You owe them and everyone around you to rise to the responsibilities of your opportunities.

In the end, we get the leaders we deserve because leaders respect what we inspect. Let's expect more from our leaders and inspect their behavior more deeply and more frequently.

As we clarify our opportunities and responsibilities as leaders we learn that our greatest lever to improve our team's performance is to be very clear about what's expected of each member of our team and their role in bringing its vision into reality.

The clarity you create and hold for your team across time will build the fetch required to do truly great things.

Further reading

- Aristotle, *Categories in Organon*, fourth century BCE
- Carlson, practiceofinnovation.com
- Descartes, *Rules for the Direction of the Mind*, 1626
- Descartes, *Discourse on the Method of Rightly Conducting One's Reason and of Seeking Truth in the Sciences*, 1637
- Hines, *Burnham of Chicago: Architect and Planner*, 1979
- George, *The Lean Six Sigma Pocket Toolbook*, 2005
- Goldratt, *The Goal*, 1984
- Gawande, *The Checklist Manifesto*, 2009
- Kreeft, *Socratic Logic*, 2004
- Kuprenas and Frederick, *101 Things I Learned in Engineering School*, 2013

- Minto, Search, "Barbara Minto McKinsey MECE" to learn the origins and intent of that method
- Nietszche, *Beyond Good and Evil*, 1886
- Pearson, "A Plantsman's Vision: Piet Oudolf," The Guardian, April 7, 2013
- Rasiel, *The McKinsey Way*, 1999

11

Humane leaders must step into the delicate moment when a person may lack the ability to perform as needed. This can be a devastating moment or one filled with grace and optimism; the humane leader will be mindful and visionary in holding this critical tipping point.

For instance, you may have a team member who is harming the psychological safety of your team. They may be unable to exercise enough self control to speak kindly to their coworkers in key moments.

Despite solemn promises and good intentions, the performance doesn't meet expectations. We have removed the M, O, and C performance variables and we're facing an issue with Ability. Now what?

When talking to the person about their attempts to succeed and the challenges they experience, you might both realize that the person does not have the talent or the tools to do the work required by the position. Then, the leader's role is to decide to either train them up or say, "Let's find you a position that works better with your skills so you can make your best contribution."

The Performance Wisdom Jig allows you to collaboratively clarify this decision in a way that is non-blaming and non-judgmental. It's just like, "Our shared analysis indicates an issue with ability. Do you agree? Then let's decide what to change to make it work better for everyone. The options are to uplevel your skills or change your role." Either way, the person gets to find a better fit, by growing or shifting responsibilities.

Extending Abilities: The Greatest Opportunity

One of the most satisfying opportunities of leadership is the extending of people's ability to contribute, one of the highest purposes of work.

We can amplify a person's ability by identifying and developing talents through training, resources and offering better tools.

Talents are either physical (agility, strength, stamina) or, increasingly in the modern world, cognitive. Improving our thinking is now a key to increased capability, productivity, and impacts.

> Man was born to be rich, or, inevitably grows rich by the use of his faculties; by the union of thought with nature. Property is an intellectual production. The game requires coolness, right reasoning, promptness, and patience in the players. Cultivated labor drives out brute labor....
>
> Wealth begins in... giving, on all sides, by tools and auxiliaries, the greatest possible extension to our powers, as if it added feet, and hands, and eyes, and blood, length to the day, and knowledge, and good–will.
>
> — Emerson, "Wealth"

Developing your team's powers of thoughtful, "cultivated" labor is your job as leader. Each team member will define "wealth" differently, but your job is to help them each find the sense of contribution and wealth they seek. In this chapter, we will address variables that leaders can control in ascending order of difficulty. We'll start with tools, then we'll move on to the identification and development of talent. And finally, we will review some thoughts on training itself.

Tools: Extending Your Team's Power

Leaders choose the tools that extend their team's native powers and talents. Just as the coach offers the equipment for practice, the leader offers the tools and the work space for the team's efforts.

First, we need a very clear understanding of how each role creates value and how tools– be they processes or technology tools, machines or information systems– extend the value creation work. Choosing the best tools requires a deep and precise understanding of the details of value creation processes we discussed in chapters eight and ten.

For now, let's agree that leaders must be looking at the value creation process continuously to anticipate the next likely constraint and begin to work on creating tools (processes and systems) to help remove it.

With these tools, it is important to design experiments to rapidly prototype and refine solutions. We should not just invest in the tool by following the herd. No, the leader's job is to deploy the capital, time and energy required to understand the costs and benefits of any new tool before asking the team to use it.

It's important to remember, the tool does not create the value, a person creates value using a process employing a tool. Processes are the methodical mental tools required to create value with systems. This will always be true until you have a completely automated value chain.

Please, let's not keep hoping a new, popular tool is the solution. Many purveyors of tools will try to tell you that the tool is the solution, but the tool is only one small piece of the solution. Be aware of the financial, control or ego biases of anyone trying to convince you otherwise. Every new tool will slow your team down before it adds value. Your job is to make sure the effort and lost productivity will be worth your team's time and frustration.

When the System is the Problem

Leaders must look and listen closely to understand the purpose and efficiency of all the systems and processes their team uses. This periodic review is required because processes and people change in ways that make systems less relevant over time and any system not creating client value drags down performance and morale.

Unfortunately, most people operating our systems are working so hard to be effective each day that they don't ask if the system is still creating client value efficiently across the entire team. So the leader needs to be the one asking the Lean method (Toyota Way) questions continuously on the team's behalf:

- **Muda**– what are we doing that is not creating value for clients?
- **Muri**– what are we doing that is simply inefficient or administrative overhead?
- **Mura**– what are we doing that is creating roughness & inefficiency (wild swings from waiting to stressed) in our process?

It's your job to ensure your systems support the value creating performance of our teams. If they do not, you must advocate for upgrading or removing systems that require too much effort.

For instance, a customer relationship management (CRM) system can be a critical tool for driving and focusing sales efforts. CRM systems are often implemented by management to track sales effort and improve the productivity and profitability of the organization's investment in sales labor.

I have seen many CRM systems implemented with this goal that actually wasted sales people's time and mental energy wading through screen after screen to enter data that only served empty reporting and accountability, not client value, salesperson efficiency, or sales growth. Sales meetings in these organizations often focus on reviewing total sales, rep activities, and deal pipeline value and velocity rather than developing the team's ability to sell more.

This is like a sports coach only looking at the scoreboard and stats sheet during a game. The game is played on the field, not on the scoreboard. Leaders need to focus on supporting the daily play by play work, position by position, to drive results. Systems need to support the success of each player as they create value for clients, not only collect data for the scoreboard. With gamification, systems can actually make creating value fun. Here, B.J. Fogg's, Persuasive Technology, has some interesting and useful first principle level ideas.

A system worthy of your team will support their most basic value creation work. For instance, the basic value creation unit of sales work is a client conversation. The CRM system should be designed to prompt the user with their next, most potentially valuable sales action (email, call, text, etc) and support their preparation for the conversation by giving them context and the focus question for the interaction. Then, as the call unfolds, the system would ideally prompt the user to create meaningful data and notes about what was learned and next steps. In the best case, the system would respond to what data had been gathered in the conversation so far and offer real time prompts to ask further questions or make certain offers while providing supporting scripts and sales materials.

After the call, the user would be encouraged by seeing their progress towards their daily and periodic goals, as well as how that relates to their own, personal goals. Creating value for clients in a system like that would be fun.

Do you see how this system would support a salesperson to use and create data that is valuable to the client and the firm **and** be encouraged to take the next steps to create even more value for themselves, their clients, and the firm? Do your systems and tools offer this level of support to your team in the critical moments of your value creation processes?

This type of system requires investment, first by the team leader and later by the firm. The team leader starts the improvement process by learning the basics of process analysis and design.

She then asks her team how the current process and system could better support their work. The leader must host this honest and open conversation, balancing the needs of the team's value creation work with the needs and constraints of the organization.

No budget is no excuse. All of your team's ideas can be ranked by level of impact and investment. Great improvements requiring little to no new investment can likely be made. Those free or low cost improvements can then be used as evidence to justify larger investments by the organization.

Small changes can also earn the team's patience as you seek the budget to make bigger improvements.

Designing the order of work to maximize impact, learning, and proof points within your constraints is the leader's responsibility, period.

Leaders Own Adoption

It's critical for leaders in modern enterprise to learn the basics of process reengineering and change management to support your team's adoption of new systems.

- Process reengineering is the art of gathering requirements for and redesigning work processes.
- Change management is the art of helping humans adapt to changes in their tools and processes.

Of course, there are entire professions organized around these topics, but a leader who doesn't educate himself in at least the first principles of those practices will be failing himself, his team and his organization.

In the end, the quality of your performance will be influenced by your employees' roles in designing and adopting the new processes and systems. The leader must understand and manage the process reengineering and change management closely to earn the team's commitment to adopting the new system.

Once the well-designed new system is fully adopted, performance will depend on the quality of the talent on your team.

Talent

We often assume that with a great job description, a good employment brand, and a strong hiring process we can almost plug and play talent into our team. When talent is not working out, you can simply replace them with fresh talent. Unfortunately, this was never quite true and is even less so in a competitive race for highly skilled labor.

In the past, many successful businesses invested in developing talent through skills and leadership development programs. But today fewer businesses are run this way. There is a trend toward using highly skilled talent to automate lower skilled work. The work of automation requires deep knowledge and specialized skills, so retaining and developing highly skilled talent over time remains critical to the organization's success.

Of course, automation of so many jobs creates societal and moral challenges we are just beginning to wrestle with. This book is aimed at equipping team leaders to support the engagement and development of valuable workers, but it is also a call for leaders to think beyond shareholder value to their larger responsibilities and possibilities. This is one of the key distinctions between humane leadership and its antithesis.

Inhumane leadership treats talent as a fungible or easily interchangeable asset. Humane leaders treat talent as an unfolding relationship to develop and engage over extended periods of time. We can think of humane leadership like nurturing trees in an organic permaculture orchard. We encourage and support their natural patterns of growth to meet our needs for fruit rather than pouring herbicides and fertilizers onto them or replacing them every few months.

Inhumane leadership begins with ideas like:

- Human resources
- Human capital
- Human assets
- Manpower (any different from horsepower?)

These models imply ownership of resources and assets by the organization, they imply utilization and optimization of return on "assets" and they lead to simplistic logic like: bring in the best talent assets, move unproductive talent along, hire more assets when you need them, pay them the least possible and manipulate behavior with incentives and corrective actions to maximize return on investment in "human capital."

Organizations with this mindset often end up with a deeply cynical culture and a workforce of people with little commitment, initiative, or imagination. Maybe the crisis of employee disengagement says more about our mental models for organizations than it does about the character of our team mates. Unfortunately, inhumane leaders keep pouring on the incentives and layers of accountability, but, mysteriously, performance never improves for long and good performers leave to find better bosses, culture and opportunities.

How did we get here?

Inhumane Leadership: The Crisis We Chose

Inhumane leadership has been a very practical approach across time. Leaders, especially in business, have been rewarded for focusing on bottom line results, limiting the scope of their own responsibility, and focusing on near term profitability rather than long-term, system-wide effects. This is a known model, it has worked for a few generations to create great material and financial wealth for many shareholders.

Unfortunately, this approach also creates organizations in which people feel exploited and have a hard time caring about the organization. As we pointed out in chapter one, Gallup has found that 70% of American workers are disengaged at work, phoning it in rather than giving their best. Manufacturing lines are one of the most efficient uses of human labor and 75% of manufacturing workers are disengaged. Workers in a hyper-automated Amazon warehouse in the UK recently reported in a survey that 89% felt exploited by the company. Amazon is a young, fairly progressive firm and still, they've structured work in the way that leaves people feeling exploited (Frontline).

Now, the questions become:

- Does your firm see people as cogs in a machine?
- If so, does that align with your values?
- If your employer doesn't share your values, why are you working there?

To improve performance, we must address the causes of disengagement, both our own and our team's. No one is more pivotal to the quality of employee engagement than their leader, you.

Humane and Sustainable

In the face of crises like low productivity and revenue growth and staff disengagement, leaders seek clear-eyed analysis on how to make hard decisions in a humane way. In seeking a sustainable path through a crisis, a humane leader will ask:

- What is the root cause of this crisis and what can we learn from it?
- What did we miss along the way that brought us to this moment?
- What did we not do that we should have done? What did we do that we should not have?
- What assumptions went into those decisions?
- What mental models led us to those decisions? What model might have worked better?
- Were we aligned with our most enlightened, deepest held values? If not, what values did we pursue and whose are they? How did we get off track?
- How do we return to what's more true and right for us and our organization?

When we look honestly at these questions, we realize that almost always the crisis was caused by a failure of leadership.

This is humbling but also empowering. Seeing the truth allows us to choose a new, truer, more sustainable path. For leaders, this can bring us to the most empowering question of all: "How would I lead myself more humanely to avoid repeating this series of misadventures?" Thus begins your new self development efforts, full of experiments and learnings.

Humane Talent Development

Humane leaders see every person on the team as a bundle of talents, developing and latent, just waiting to find ways to grow and create more value.

Talents may be given as gifts of birth, but they all require development through practice, refinement and more practice. Even with great tools, people need well-developed talents to create all the value they might contribute.

Hiring processes typically aim to hire well-developed talent, therefore the focus on resumes, vetting, and pay based on work experience. Proven talent is expensive and less risky, while latent talent– as in recent college graduates– generally gets paid less, but suffers from higher turnover rates.

As leaders, we can benefit from discovering and developing talent that may not yet be obvious to others. Orchardists don't transplant mature trees, they plant and nurture tiny seedlings to build fruitfulness over time.

No one on your team is fully developed, no matter their age or experience level. So talent development becomes a key contribution you can make to your team and organization. This approach to talent development fulfills all the promises of this book: it engages, empowers, and improves the performance of your team members.

For example, I once led a project to merge three sales and order management systems into one and radically streamline a complex order entry process. As we announced the project, I noticed our most skilled and experienced team members rolling their eyes and shooting each other skeptical glances. They asked a couple of polite, but pointed questions, and I knew there was an iceberg of change management and adoption challenges under the smiling doubts they'd revealed.

I could have dismissed them as laggards, luddites, know-it-alls, or complainers. Fortunately, I knew them to be thoughtful, committed, talented women. After the meeting, I called them into my office.

I said, "I need you and all of your doubts and concerns. You are critical to the success of this project." It was June and we had only three months to get the new system designed, developed and tested before all software changes would be locked down company-wide. In the fall we'd have 150 people, most of them seasonal new hires, working in the system, so it had to be bulletproof. The skeptic's job was to identify every requirement, potential point of failure, and every bug before we had to lock the code. They became my requirements building and testing team, a challenging role with far more responsibility than they'd had before.

As we designed the system, I adjusted their daily responsibilities to allow them to work as a team. We taught them how to identify key process and system requirements, run tests in the processes and software, record bugs, and work with our developer on refinements. Much to their credit, no one noticed that we completely reengineered the sales and order entry process when the flood of holiday orders washed through. Their experience, augmented by their new skills and responsibilities, averted multiple potential disasters.

As a leader, it's critical to map people into opportunities for them to learn how to contribute in new ways. If you have the map of your team's value creation process you created based on your work in chapter eight, you can now enrich it by adding roles, people and their talents.

- How well do the roles, people, and their talents line up?
- Do roles need to be clarified or redefined?
- Could tasks be more precisely and flexibly mapped to meet the team's talents?
- Are talents required that don't yet exist on the team?
- Do critical steps in your value creation process all hinge on one person's talent? How risky is that?
- How can you build redundancy and resilience by developing some of the talents of others on the team?
- How is team performance being limited by a lack of talent in one or more members of the team?

Use this enriched value creation map to identify opportunities to build your team's skills, engagement and resilience. This map is your ticket to deep fulfillment. Leaders often look back at developing a person's latent talents as the greatest achievement and most satisfying outcome of their careers.

Training that Fits

Learning happens best when we feel an immediate need. The connection of lesson to practical application creates genuine curiosity, and a desire to perform better.

I would caution against thinking that occasional packaged online or workshop training programs are enough to optimally develop your team's talents. Deep, sustainable improvements in skills, especially complex or soft skills, require not only more investment of time and attention but also an easily accessible, well-organized and searchable library of training materials relevant to your team's key value creation roles. Once built, this library allows the leader to co-curate development roadmaps for each team member. The leader becomes like a reference librarian connecting people with the content that best serves their curiosity.

- What training is relevant for you today?
- Do you have the time and focus to optimally develop your skills?
- Do you have related work to give you immediate experience with your new skills?

Here's an easy learning and development roadmap that works from the felt need for some improvement. Felt need might arise from a desire to learn new things, a performance improvement experiment, or simply frustration. The roadmap then tracks the skills to develop and holds accountability for measurable improvements on a clear timeline.

Skills development roadmap example:

Skills to Develop

Felt Need	Skills to Develop	Measure of Improved Skill (Speed, Accuracy, Output)	Date Done

Development Road Map to Root Training Efforts in Time

Skills to Develop	Year			
	Q1	Q2	Q3	Q4

Download a template for this Development Roadmap Wisdom Jig from the Humane Leadership website.

Collaborating with each of your team members to create a clear, methodical approach to increasing their capacity to create client value creation is a gift to everyone involved.

But, learning and development takes time and a focus on performance just like any other activity.

Improving Training Performance

If we want our team members to perform well at improving their skills, we can apply the P(MOCA) performance model to training itself.

- **Motivation**– the personal and professional felt needs for training.
- **Opportunity**– time to really dig in, deeply learn, and practice.
- **Clarity**– what training outcomes are relevant now.
- **Ability**– a library of learning tools and training materials.

But, performance, even in learning, requires fetch. Once you have identified the roadmap for each person, you need to have it on your agenda for all your upcoming 1:1 meetings. We ask, "Please show me your progress on your learning and development roadmap" to close the loop. Closing the loop will accomplish three important goals: First, it will teach them to respect the map of their own development; people respect what you inspect.

Second, it will convince them that their development is routine and inevitable in your mind. You will not forget about their learning because you are committed to their development over time. Leaders are often the ones who hold faith in a person's talent and development earlier and longer than the person does themselves.

Third, the closed loop of roadmap and learning is habit forming. Each success builds the learning habit by giving the person a healthy reward loop. You are literally building positive addictions to learning by creating rewarding experiences for them.

This is how you can build habits and culture at the brain chemistry level that will serve you and your team for a lifetime. More on this in a bit.

Just a note here that training does not need to be expensive and time consuming. In fact, some of the most effective training is very short and homegrown, as long as it is well linked to the felt needs of the moment and available on demand.

Tailor Your Own Trainings

It is possible that the most relevant source of new training materials are your current team members. Some of them have refined very specific skills that create great value for your clients and organization. Your job is to find, record, and amplify those ideas and voices. Find the person who is really good at a core function and help them create a simple training video on their methods.

We create training videos for clients using meeting software that allows screen sharing and video recording (we use Zoom). Here's how:

I make a quick note to myself of the key skills or tricks I want to share in the video to serve as an outline and stick it to my monitor. If you have a lot to cover, err on the side of creating more, shorter videos rather than long ones.

I open all the software, slides, documents or urls I want to show and I start a meeting with me as the only attendee.

I start recording and I offer a quick, warm greeting, explain context, the goals of the video, and very quickly explain the desired learning outcomes.

I then turn on the screen share and I do a voice over explanation as I'm showing the skills I want to teach. Lesson content can be a live demonstration of a tool you are teaching, simple presentation slides, or photos.

Once I cover all the points on my outline, I turn off screen sharing and offer advice on next steps to cement the lesson, related lessons, and other encouragements to continue learning.

I then turn off the recording and end the meeting.

Once the file converts and saves to my computer, I trim anything extra at the beginning or end, add intros or outros if I feel that's helpful and save the finalized video file.

I then upload the video file (MP4 if you are using Zoom) to YouTube as an unlisted, but shareable video lesson.

Once the video is published, I email out the link to the video to those who need it immediately and I add it to the relevant training materials index files on our intranet or training documents.

These directory documents make all of the training materials indexed by role, function, or process and easily searchable. Finding the material you need quickly is the key to on-demand training, so use all the relevant keywords you can in the filenames of these documents. If you have a large library of videos, consider using a platform like Degreed to organize and present content to your teams.

I find it useful to organize the training materials by process and organize the training index document in the same flow as your process. This allows users to use a standard mental map of your processes to find training materials related to their needs.

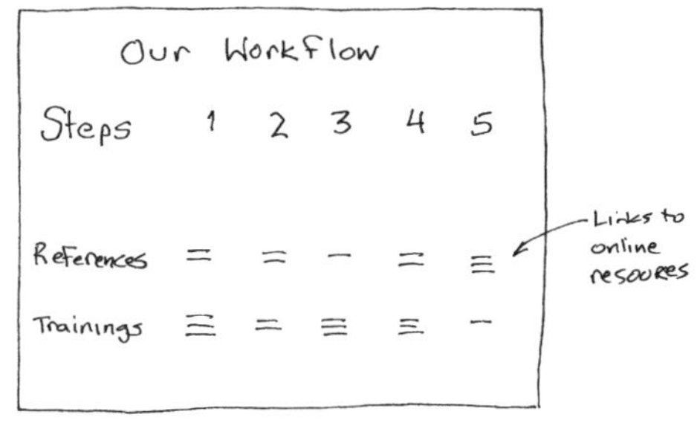

Because learning requires repetition, these video assets also allow users who need some repeats to really internalize the skill in a quiet, private way to develop themselves at their own pace.

If you are not already doing this, please don't underestimate the power of this deceptively simple idea. When used well, these internally crafted videos can transform your reach as a humane leader and radically enhance your team's ability to create client value. It also deeply engages and honors your best workers while creating a culture of innovation, sharing, and continuous development. The key is that you are enabling your team to train themselves at the moment of their need and availability.

Humane leaders help their team members light their own fires and offer them lots of fuel to keep them lit. It's not that we are offloading responsibility for development to the individuals, it's that the humane leader facilitates the individual's work to develop themselves.

> Education is not the filling of a pail, but the lighting of a fire.
>
> — Plutarch

Growing Together

There are two parties involved in the dance of learning and development, the learner and leader.

Leading by example comes first. If we become the average of the five people we spend the most time with, then leaders should strive to be a person who raises the average of the people they work with each day. In the classical world, this was called exemplum or moral example.

Plutarch, a Roman statesman and writer of the first century of the common era, wrote that humans were mixes of reason, emotion and habits that could be improved with sufficiently thoughtful and dedicated self development. A critical element of his vision were carefully selected role models, both alive and passed, to emulate. To offer these exemplum, Plutarch wrote a collection of biographies called Lives of the Noble Greeks and Romans (or Parallel Lives). Of course, today we have many more living examples, TED talks, and a huge number of other online resources. Nonetheless, the quality of the people in Plutarch's biographies made them useful over thousands of years and they remain useful today.

Once a leader sets an excellent example with her own self development, she can nurture a culture that makes learning like breathing– a natural, continuous element of our daily lives. The leader creates a learning culture by constantly learning herself, exploring the tools her team uses, new potential tools, and skills and techniques related to her own and her team's work.

But, you must be a careful curator. Some leaders assume that every new book they read or tool they discover should be pushed upon the team as a silver bullet solution. While this might feel exciting and like good intellectual leadership, it often backfires by making the leader seem unhinged from the realities of the team's daily work.

Curation is the heart of good teaching. Only offer what you have already proven is valuable in your own experience and will be easily adopted by your team. Leaders must help control the team's cognitive load over time so people are not bored or overwhelmed with the pace of change.

If you find a great idea, ask one or two people on your team if it is relevant to them. If those test pilots find the idea useful, create a short training video on the idea to share with the rest of your team.

Leaders cannot teach people who do not want to learn. To be motivated to learn, a person must first have a commitment to their own personal and professional development. If that commitment is missing, we must see if there is a lack of hope in the person. If a source of hope is nowhere to be found, we will first need to help them regain the sense of personal agency and possibility that underlie hope. This has been described in chapter seven on Roots of Motivation.

Other team members who lack humility may suffer from the illusion that they already know everything they need to know. Generally, this is fairly easy to influence given that a few simple questions can lead them back to epistemological humility (humility about the true extent of our knowledge). In the long run, we all must live in epistemological humility or we become insufferable.

Once hope and humility are established, the individual must find some source of personal curiosity. Curiosity is one of the most beautiful sources of motivation available to humans if it is directed creatively and consciously using the learning and development roadmap.

> The world is full of magical things patiently waiting for our wits to grow sharper.
>
> — Bertrand Russell

Knowing is Good, Not Knowing is Even Better

The leader's job is to create a culture of ongoing learning where it's okay to ask questions and where it's okay not to know, for now. The key is to turn the humility of not knowing into the fire of curiosity, experimentation, and sharing of discoveries. In fact, scientific communities are, ideally, just that.

As leaders of these scientifically learning communities, we become lab directors helping our team search for the best ways to create value for clients and the firm. One day the Lab Notebook might become the must-have item on your team. You can find a template on our Wisdom Jigs web page.

> Satisfaction of one's curiosity is one of the greatest sources of happiness in life.
>
> — Linus Pauling, Winner of the Nobel Peace Prize and the Nobel Prize for Chemistry

The warming fire of curiosity is a sign of a humane leader's success at creating a living, productive learning culture. To bring that culture to life, we need to create autodidacts.

Autodidacts are the Future

An autodidact is somebody who teaches themselves. By creating the roadmap and creating dopamine reward loops for ourselves, we are well on our way.

You may notice that the very best contributors in your organization today are probably people addicted to learning; they're always looking further and deeper, bringing in fresh ideas from outside, always experimenting. They're trying things in new ways, and when something works, they share their findings.

Autodidacts are the people we all want on our teams.

Leaders can build a learning culture by empowering these autodidacts by having them share what they've learned in your online collaboration environment or in meetings. They can be your star authors and librarians who are collecting and creating next level training materials.

With all its successes and challenges, Amazon is still one of the best learning cultures I know of. In their 13 management principles, "Learn and Be Curious" comes just after "Be Right, A Lot." Amazon responds seriously to errors large– taking Amazon Web Services down for a day– and small– temporary latency (slowness) impacting customers. The engineer most closely associated with the error must complete a detailed (sometimes weeks long) post-mortem report including analysis of customer impact, root causes, blast radius, event duration, health and diagnostic metrics, and how to avoid repeating the error in the future. These Correction of Error reports are widely distributed within the company and must be publicly defended in weekly operational leadership meetings before they are distributed across relevant teams in the company.

> There is no compression algorithm for experience.
>
> — Werner Vogels, CTO, Amazon

Amazon squeezes every error to extract and institutionalize all the learning possible.

To lead by example you may need to upgrade your own curiosity and study habits to become the Autodidact in Chief or Chief Curiosity Officer for your team.

Imagine the end of your career with the team that you've worked with for so long because they've been so engaged, so loyal, and having so much fun together. You look back and you see this cascade of people who have learned together and taught each other and expanded their ability to contribute not only at the office, but in the world, in a thousand different ways. To me, that sounds like a life well lived, a community and a career well built.

Further Reading

- *Frontline: Amazon Empire*, PBS, 2020
- Plutarch, *Parallel Lives,* first century CE
- Russell, *The Conquest of Happiness,* 1930
- Weiss, Amazon's approach to failing successfully (DOP208-R1) on YouTube, 2019

12

What This Means to You

I have wonderful and challenging news here at the end of our journey.

First, the wonderful news is that now you know.

You can see opportunities to become a more effective, more humane leader. You have many tools at your disposal, and you have guideposts to help you along the way. You will find challenging moments, but you will not be alone. You will find moments of exaltation that will be of your own creation. Enjoy the fruit of your labors.

The challenging news is that now you know.

Your knowing calls you to a higher level of intention and integrity in your leadership, in your thoughts and in your behavior every day. You will be called to render higher service to those around you, to your organization, to your community and even to the Earth. You have everything you need to contribute.

Leadership: A Moral Challenge

As your authority grows, you must balance creating results with moral responsibility. To do that, ground your use of power in experimentation, humility, and cooperation.

In moments of challenging edge cases, remember that useful wisdom has been explored, captured, and refined for you across the ages by people facing similar demands. Go to the library, search the web's brighter corners, ask your wisest friends. Follow every promising pathway until you find the person, the ideas, and the inspiration you need. Then, choose the next step that's aligned with your highest values and the resonant wisdom you have found.

You can lead humanely with your choices person by person, interaction by interaction, moment by moment, every day.

These choices define not only the culture of our teams and organizations but they also define your personal integrity.

> We have grasped the mystery of the atom and rejected the Sermon on the Mount.
>
> The world has achieved brilliance without conscience. Ours is a world of nuclear giants and ethical infants.
>
> — General Omar Bradley

Free Will and Consequences

St. Augustine wrote,

> We use our freedom properly when we act virtuously; we misuse it when we choose to act viciously. The will is then truly free, when it is not the slave to vices and sins.

We must choose. Not choosing the values you live by allows a master to choose you. This question of choosing which master to serve is a life-long ethical question with moment-by-moment consequences.

A person governed by passions is in

> ...bondage, for a man under their control is not his own master, but is mastered by fortune, in whose power he is. So that he is often forced to follow to the worse, although he sees the better before him.
>
> — Spinoza

When guided by these passions, we do whatever we desire or think we can get away with. That's the law of the jungle and Machiavellian politics.

We can rationalize our actions with profit seeking, ego needs, or efficiency, but there are always consequences. We experience a corruption of the spirit when we pursue moral freedom while enslaved by our baser instincts. Marlow describes Captain Kurtz in Conrad's novella, *Heart of Darkness* facing the consequences of his expedient and ego-centric moral choices:

> Anything approaching the change that came over his features I have never seen before, and hope never to see again. Oh, I wasn't touched. I was fascinated. It was as though a veil had been rent.
>
> I saw on that ivory face the expression of sombre pride, of ruthless power, of craven terror– of an intense and hopeless despair. Did he live his life again in every detail of desire, temptation, and surrender during that supreme moment of complete knowledge?
>
> He cried in a whisper at some image, at some vision– he cried out twice, a cry that was no more than a breath:
>
> "The horror! The horror!"

It's been said that power corrupts, but maybe it is our lack of courageous self leadership that allows corruption in. In moments of moral ambiguity, you might be tempted to leave the moral clarity of your values and explore the depths of a dark sea. I am reminded of a few lines from a novel:

> Consider the subtleness of the sea; how its most dreaded creatures glide under water, unapparent for the most part, and treacherously hidden beneath the loveliest tints of azure.
>
> Consider also the devilish brilliance and beauty of many of its most remorseless tribes, as the dainty embellished shape of many species of sharks.

> Consider once more, the universal cannibalism of the sea; all whose creatures prey upon each other, carrying on eternal war since the world began.
>
> Consider all this; and then turn to this green, gentle, and most docile earth; consider them both, the sea and the land; and do you not find a strange analogy to something in yourself?
>
> For as this appalling ocean surrounds the verdant land, so in the soul of man there lies one insular Tahiti, full of peace and joy, but encompassed by all the horrors of the half known life.
>
> God keep thee! Push not off from that isle, thou canst never return!
>
> — Melville, *Moby Dick*

Our Docile, Gentle Isle

You can choose to live the humane leadership values to remain on your "insular Tahiti" of the soul and one day become an exemplar of virtue. But, sometimes, we're not given the choice.

My mother, grandparents and aunt left their comfortable lives in Hungary just ahead of the fighting in October 1944 and traveled through Germany in the final months of World War Two.

I am viscerally, even epigenetically, aware that terrible things happen. My family was lucky to survive and immigrate to the United States years later, while many millions did not survive that series of horrors.

My hope is that together we can create more humane leaders who will use their freedom and power to prevent future man-made tragedies.

Freedom, to whatever extent we can achieve it, springs from our commitment to reason. As Spinoza points out in *Ethics*, when a person is governed by reason he is free, for he

> ...does the will of no one but himself, and does those things only which he knows are of greatest importance in life, and which he therefore desires above all things."

The key is to use our deepest sense of humanity in deciding what's of greatest importance. The humane leadership values can help you make those choices. So, please, be fair with your strength, generous with your care, and wise in your balance in each moment you are given to lead yourself and others.

Next Step: Global Movement In Arm's Reach

As you begin work in your self leadership lab, your engagement and empowerment will grow. When should you reach outside of your self leadership lab and start changing the world around you?

As you work with Humane Leadership practices/tools, you will begin noticing others reacting to the fruits of your new self leadership style and ask about it; then you know you are ready.

When you are ready, how far shall you reach with your leadership? Start within arm's reach, then feel the pull as others begin to see you. The pull will make you aware of the wisdom of your balance and the fairness of your strength.

Recently, I realized that everything I need to be a good leader and to live a high-quality, purposeful life is within arm's reach. Everybody I need to touch, everything I need to change, every resource is likely close at hand if I just look and listen more closely and think a bit more creatively.

This is not because I live in the center of the universe, but because change happens one person at a time. Any good we create in relationship with another ripples outward.

In this rippling, I have great faith. I am not the only one who believes this; Zappo's entire business plan was focused on creating amazing customer service experiences one person at a time with no marketing budget beyond taking care of the humans who ask for help. Of course, technology lets thousands see us every day. Good deeds and clear ideas spread quickly in our networked world.

If you have a team now, you can start creating humane leadership experiences immediately. Ask your team members fresh questions and look at them with fresh eyes. Be with them in a more curious and open way. Note their successes and challenges, offer them options and tools that have been helpful to you in your self leadership practice. Watch to see if positive change starts to happen for them. As you see change, take a moment to appreciate and amplify it.

The key is to **see.**

> When in the course of human events, it becomes necessary for one people…
>
> to fulfill the promise of being one people, necessary to abolish any government that becomes destructive of these ends, necessary to dissolve the political bans that keep us from speaking to each other, necessary to avow our interdependence, to look straight into each other's eyes the way we behold the moon, and declare to one another: I see you. I see you. I see you.
>
> — Richard Blanco, "Declaration of Inter-Dependence"

Just seeing others will engage and empower them. Seeing ourselves and others as creators of change in the world empowers us and ripples out to everyone around us.

Be The Change

Influence the world by being the leader you want to follow.

By leading ourselves more humanely, we begin to shift the global culture of leadership by healing one relationship, one team, one organization at a time.

I am excited to live in a future rising from humane leadership values. A future that welcomes a rising tide of diverse, growing leaders who:

- Know and heal themselves
- Empower others
- Accept responsibility

- Welcome accountability

I want to live in **that** future.

Please start where you are, you'll be surprised as every aspect of your life transforms. Your transformation will inspire others to join you.

This Ending is Your Daily Beginning

Your humane leadership path unfolds day by day. The path from here invites you to embrace a new life.

> I left the woods for as good a reason as I went there.
>
> Perhaps it seemed to me that I had several more lives to live, and could not spare any more time for that one.
>
> It is remarkable how easily and insensibly we fall into a particular route, and make a beaten track for ourselves.
>
> ...The surface of the earth is soft and impressible by the feet of men; and so with the paths which the mind travels. How worn and dusty, then, must be the Highways of the world, how deep the ruts of tradition and conformity!
>
> I did not wish to take a cabin passage [comfortable inside a ship], but rather to go before the mast and on the deck of the world, for there I could best see the moonlight amid the mountains. I do not wish to go below now.

> I learned this, at least, by my experiment: that if one advances confidently in the direction of his dreams, and endeavors to live the life which he has imagined, he will meet with a success unexpected in common hours.
>
> He will put some things behind, will pass an invisible boundary; new, universal, and more liberal laws will begin to establish themselves around and within him;
>
> ...If you have built castles in the air, your work need not be lost; that is where they should be. Now put the foundations under them.
>
> — Thoreau, *Walden*

I join you in building what's new, stone by stone, choice by choice, now, and again, now.

Further Reading

I hope that you will follow the further reading invitations throughout the book to greater curiosity, humility, compassion, and wisdom on your leadership journey.

- Blanco, *How to Love a Country*, 2019
- Conrad, *Heart of Darkness*, 1902
- Melville, *Moby Dick*, 1851, quote from chapter 58
- Spinoza, *Ethics*, 1677
- Thoreau, *Walden*, 1854

Epilogue

I See You

About the little girl in the epigraph; what she meant to me and might mean to you.

One morning in early October 1987, I encountered a tiny infant girl on a sidewalk in Mumbai, India. She sat at the very edge of a busy road amidst shards of broken glass, flies on her face. She looked up at me as her mother sorted a pile of garbage nearby.

My heart broke in her gaze and everything I had trained my mind to think about life and opportunity shattered and fell to the ground.

In my self absorbed youthfulness, I thought that I could or should save her. But I could not take her away and I knew that there were tens of millions of children like her even if I did help her.

But how could I walk away and leave her sitting in the perilous fate of her birth?

Before I could turn away, I naively vowed to myself to use my life's many privileges and blessings in her honor.

Just being, she called me to be a leader of a different kind.

She is the one who invented humane leadership by planting a seed of compassion within me. That seed shattered the ideas that kept me from seeing other humans clearly and carefully. That seed continued to grow, sometimes uncomfortably, within me.

She made it impossible for me to pursue wealth, fame, or power for their own sake. As I extend my compassion to those suffering in poverty around the less developed world, I also feel compassion for humans in developed nations who suffer from poverty of hope, empowerment, and imagination.

Now, I hope that you will join me in honoring the suffering of all people by consciously choosing to lead from whatever privilege you have. Each of us has some shred of free will within arm's reach.

Our job as self leaders is to create opportunities for ourselves and for millions of people like us to think and act freely from our ethical values.

If we try alone, it feels hopeless. If we try together, it feels possible.

So leader, I look forward to connecting with you, to hearing of your journey, to learning from you, to creating a vision together, and to rising and setting to work in building the foundations under our dreams of a brighter shared future.

Namaste,

Stephen

Acknowledgements

This project was made possible by all the teammates and clients who bumped along with me and sometimes suffered as I learned first about leading, then about humanity.

I thank my partner and gifted, saintly editor, Ellie Holty.

Of course I thank my children for their forbearance as I plowed months into building this book, time that could have been spent hiking, skiing and laughing a bit more with them. I thank my parents for creating so many windows of opportunity for me over the years. I thank Luna Alvarez for being a fearless test pilot in reading the manuscript.

I thank all of my teachers in this adventure:

- The fellow travellers seeking a more compassionate, mindful and ethical way of leading ourselves and each other
- All the lovers of wisdom who took the time to write down their best thoughts over the years
- My business mentors from the early days, Peter Sloan and Glen Christensen
- My early writing and thinking mentors Mary Yeager and Thomas Hines at UCLA
- My Master Coach and friend, Molly Gordon, who started me on the path of serving leaders by calling me out of retirement to ask if I might consider helping a business owner she knew

And, I thank you for paying attention to what's right and what's possible.